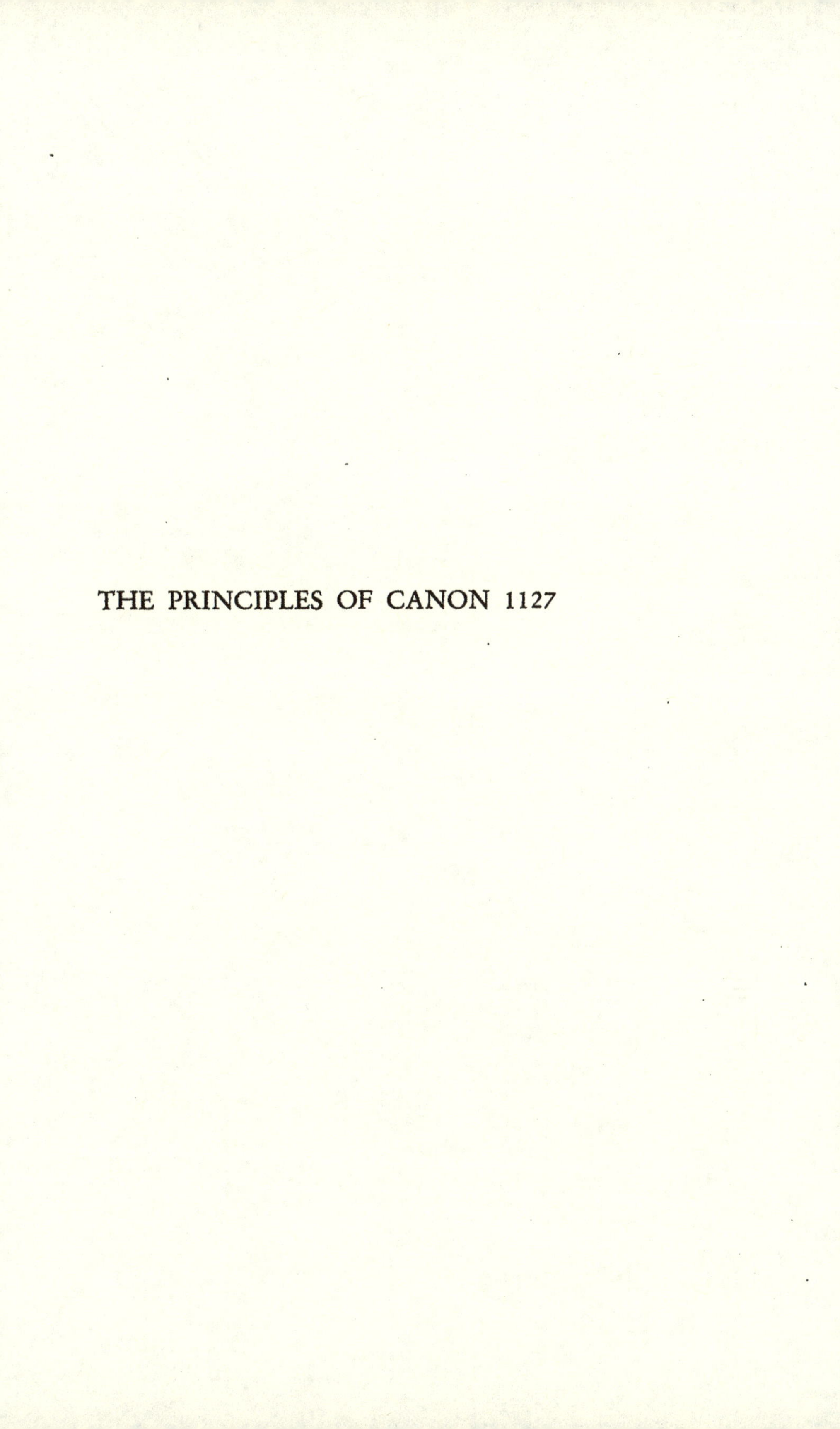

THE PRINCIPLES OF CANON 1127

THE CATHOLIC UNIVERSITY OF AMERICA
CANON LAW STUDIES
No. 163

THE PRINCIPLES OF CANON 1127

A DISSERTATION

BY

FRANCIS PATRICK KEARNEY, A.B., S.T.L., J.C.L.

Priest of the Archdiocese of Baltimore

Submitted to the Faculty of Canon Law of the Catholic University of America in Partial Fulfillment of the Requirements for the Degree of

DOCTOR OF CANON LAW

THE CATHOLIC UNIVERSITY OF AMERICA PRESS
WASHINGTON, D. C.
1942

NIHIL OBSTAT:

CLEMENS V. BASTNAGEL, J.U.D., S.T.L.,
Censor Deputatus.

Washingtonii, D. C., die 29 maii, 1942.

IMPRIMATUR:

✠ MICHAEL J. CURLEY, D.D.,
Archiepiscopus Baltimorensis et Washingtonensis.

Baltimorae, Md., die 6 iunii, 1942.

PRINTED IN THE UNITED STATES OF AMERICA
BY THE WATKINS PRINTING CO., BALTIMORE

TO MY MOTHER AND FATHER

AND TO M. G. M.

TABLE OF CONTENTS

FOREWORD

Canon 1127, "In doubtful matters the privilege of the faith enjoys the favor of the law," embodies a juridical principle of great latitude. That this principle may be of practical importance not in mission territories alone but in the United States as well, is not at all surprising. Reliable statistics gathered by the United States Bureau of Census show that one divorce is granted for every five marriages contracted. Many of these divorces affect those who either certainly are not baptized or those in whose case the validity of baptism is open to serious question. The privilege of the faith, applied according to the norm of canon 1127, may offer a solution to the otherwise insoluble matrimonial problems which arise upon the conversion of such non-Catholics who, after obtaining civil divorces, have attempted or wish to contract new marriages.

Despite this importance the historical development and the practical application of canon 1127 have been, to a large extent, neglected by modern canonists. The principle of this canon represents no innovation in ecclesiastical jurisprudence. There is no doubt that the legal phraseology in which the canon is cast is traceable directly to a letter of Benedict XIV, in which he determined that the welfare of the faith should always determine the decision of doubtful matters. This general principle is taken up in canon 1127 and applied specifically to all cases wherein the continuation or the maintenance of a marriage which was contracted in infidelity would prove an obstacle to the acquisition or the profession of the Catholic Faith.

The Holy Office has frequently applied this principle as a safe rule of practical action to resolve doubts about the validity of a marriage contracted in infidelity, or about the application of the Pauline Privilege, when the essential conditions were but doubtfully fulfilled and the conversion to the faith depended on the solution of such problems.

This study of canon 1127 will attempt to trace the history of the general principle that in doubtful matters the privilege of the faith enjoys the favor of the law as well as the specific application of this principle to the dissolution of the bond of legitimate marriage. The

Canonical Commentary will attempt to clarify the practical application of canon 1127 in the light of its historical background, if the decisions of the Holy See and if the interpretation of canonists, with reference to the cases in which the conditions for the application of the privilege of the faith are but doubtfully fulfilled. It need hardly be emphasized that the writer's preoccupation has been to indicate the manner in which canon 1127 may be applied by the local ordinary and by other persons inferior to the Holy See.

The writer takes this occasion to offer his sincere thanks to His Excellency, the Most Reverend Michael J. Curley, D.D., for the opportunity of graduate study in Canon Law; to the members of the Faculty of the School of Canon Law for their help and kindness during the preparation of the work; to M. G. M. and to many others whose generous assistance made this dissertation possible.

PART ONE

HISTORICAL DEVELOPMENT

CHAPTER I

PRELIMINARY DISCUSSION

ARTICLE I. DEFINITION OF TERMS OF CANON 1127

In Re Dubia Privilegium Fidei Gaudet Favore Iuris.

To avoid confusion in attempting to trace the historical development of canon 1127, it is necessary at the outset to determine the meaning of the terms employed in the phrasing of the canon. Such a determination must, as is evident, embrace three elements: the notion of the privilege of the faith; the notion of the favor of the law; the notion of doubtful matters. The immediately following treatment is not intended to be a strict canonical commentary, but rather a clarification of the object of an inquiry into the historical development of the principle that "in doubtful matters the privilege of the faith enjoys the favor of the law."

A. *The Privilege of the Faith*

Modern canonical usage attributes to the term "privilege of the faith" a threefold signification. It may be understood as a broad, general principle conferring the right to choose in doubtful cases that probable solution which will be favorable to the acquisition or the conservation of the faith.[1] But canon 1127, by its position in the Code, has a specific application to matrimonial problems. Thus the privilege of the faith in canon 1127 may refer to any judgment made in favor of the faith whereby a marriage of doubtful validity is judged and considered either as valid or as invalid according as that

[1] Cappello, *Tractatus Canonico-Moralis de Sacramentis* (3 vols. in 6, Vol. III, *De Matrimonio*, 4. ed., Taurinorum Augustae: Marietti, 1939), III, n. 788, nota 75; Louis Chaussegros de Léry, *Le Privilège de la Foi* (Montreal: Collection des Studia, 1938), n. 1; Creusen, "Baptême Douteux et Mariage Indissoluble,"—*Nouvelle Revue Théologique*, LII (1925), 229. Hereafter *NRT*. See also *infra*, Article II; Chapter II.

validity or invalidity opens the way for conversion to the faith and the reception of baptism.[2]

In its strictest sense the privilege of the faith signifies the faculty granted to a convert from infidelity, through power divinely besowed, whereby, after the reception of baptism, the convert may contract a second marriage if the infidel consort departs. This is the sense in which the privilege of the faith is most commonly used and, as such, it is synonymous with the Pauline Privilege. Certainly canon 1127 refers at least to the privilege of the faith so understood.

But, in relation to marriage problems, this term has been broadened to include the power of the Pope over consummated, legitimate marriages, when at least one party to such a marriage has been converted and the good of the faith demands the dissolution of a bond contracted in infidelity. The existence and the use of such power is evident from the provisions of canon 1125 and from the dissolution of the natural bond of marriage as granted in what has become known as the Helena Case.[3] From this it appears that the privilege of the faith referred to in canon 1127 is a genus of which the Pauline Privilege is a species; and that canon 1127 may be applied to the fullest extent of the term.[4]

B. *The Favor of the Law*

The term "favor of the law," considered objectively as found in canon 1127, signifies the inclination of the legislator to admit the use

[2] S.C.S. Off. (Siouxormen.) 18 maii 1892, ad 2—*Codicis Iuris Canonici Fontes Cura Emi. Petri Card. Gasparri Editi,* 9 vols., Romae (postea Civitate Vaticana): Typis Polyglottis Vaticanis, 1923-1939. (Vols. VII, VIII et IX ed. cura et studio Emi. Iustiniani Card. Seredi). n. 1155. Hereafter *Fontes.* Vromant, *Facultates Quas S. C. Prop. Fide Delegare Solet Ordinariis Missionum, Commentaria in Formulam Tertiam* (Louvain, 1926), n. 83; Vermeersch, *De Casu Apostoli* (Brugis, 1911), n. 31.

[3] *ER,* LXXII (1925), 186-188; Bouscaren, *Canon Law Digest* (2 Vols. and Supplement—1941, Milwaukee: Bruce, 1934-1941), I, 552, 553.

[4] Cf. *infra,* Chapter V; Cappello, *De Matrimonio,* III, n. 788; Arendt, "Quomodo in favorem fidei solvatur a S. Pontifice matrimonium in infidelitate contractum, Nota theologico-canonica circa canonem 1127,"—*Ephemerides Theologicae Lovanienses,* I (1924), 184. Hereafter "Nota circa canonem 1127,"—*ETL.*

of the privilege of the faith in a doubtful matter. Canon 1014 establishes the general presumption of the validity of marriage by granting it the favor of the law. It makes an exception, however, for canon 1127. The presumption in favor of the validity of marriage, which is to be upheld in doubt both of law and of fact, yields to the presumption in favor of the faith or to the liberty of a convert from infidelity.[5]

C. *Doubtful Matters*

In the present treatment of the term "*in re dubia*" of canon 1127 it is intended only to indicate that the doubtful matters referred to will concern the verification of the conditions necessary for the application of the privilege of the faith. The determination of the nature of the doubt required for the application of canon 1127, the necessity of a meticulous examination to demonstrate that the doubt is morally insoluble, and the specific enumeration of matters which may remain doubtful in this sense, belong properly to the canonical commentary and will be there fully treated.[6] The doubtful matters contemplated in canon 1127 will be, for example, the existence of the validity of a marriage contracted in infidelity; the dissolution of a marriage contracted in infidelity or the fulfillment of the requirements essential for the use of the Pauline Privilege.

Article II. General Notes on the History of the Privilege of the Faith

The historical development of canon 1127 in its bearing on matrimonial problems must of necessity be concomitant with the development of the Pauline Privilege. Marriage contracted in infidelity, when only one party was later converted, from the earliest days of the Church caused difficulties which evoked the application of the Pauline Privilege. The first four centuries of church history attest to the continued necessity and practical utility of this juridical institution.

[5] S.C.S. Off., instr. (ad Ep. S. Alberti), 9 dec. 1874—*Fontes*, n. 1036; S.C.S. Off., instr. (ad Vic. Ap. Oceaniae Central.), 18 dec. 1872—*Fontes*, n. 1024.

[6] Cf. *infra*, Chapter V, p. 49.

With the spiritual triumph on the part of Christianity during the succeeding centuries, and with the isolation of the Jewish population as foreign colonies in Christian states, the urgent need of the Pauline Privilege declined. But, following the great geographical discoveries of the sixteenth and seventeenth centuries, the privilege found a vast field of application in newly opened mission countries. Indeed, the difficulties encountered in these missions, caused by the prevalent practice of polygamy among the infidel population, occasioned the exercise of the supreme ministerial power of the Sovereign Pontiff to dissolve the bond of infidel marriage, upon the conversion of at least one party in such a marriage. Here was laid the foundation of canon 1127. The decisions and instructions of the Holy Office during the eighteenth and nineteenth centuries repeated frequently the principle of this canon, namely, that in doubtful matters the privilege of the faith enjoys the favor of the law. Such, in brief, are the lines of development that a history of canon 1127 must follow.

The general principle of which canon 1127 is an application, that in doubtful matters it is a constant rule that the judgment should favor the faith, was framed by Benedict XIV.[7] To trace every instance in which this principle has been applied in ecclesiastical jurisprudence would be evidently impossible. It is but consonant with the mission of the Church that the Pope do all in his power to promote the welfare of the faith and to remove obstacles to conversion. The present study, therefore, attempts in its historical conspectus merely to present those instances of the application of this general principle which guided Benedict XIV in his statement of it and to show the direct relationship which it bears to the principle of canon 1127.

[7] *Probe te*, 15 dec. 1751, ad 27: "In re dubia in favorem fidei pronuntiandum esse constans regula est."—*Fontes*, n. 418.

CHAPTER II

THE PRIVILEGE OF THE FAITH AS A GENERAL PRINCIPLE

In commenting on the principle contained in canon 1127, canonists regard it as a particular application of a general rule first clearly enunciated by Benedict XIV.[1] In this letter Benedict XIV declared that the baptism of a child presented by a Catholic grandmother, in spite of the opposition of the child's Jewish mother, could be legitimately administered. The right of the Catholic grandmother, in such a case, was of a doubtful character. Benedict XIV solved the doubt in favor of the true faith and stated that it was a constant rule in doubtful matters to pronounce in favor of the faith. Wernz-Vidal [2] question the applicability of this principle to the solution of doubts in regard to marriages contracted in infidelity, for Benedict XIV had a matter entirely different in mind. That, of course, was quite true; but Benedict stated a *general* principle which he considered well established, not one which he was introducing into ecclesiastical jurisprudence.

Certainly it is but consistent with the divine mission entrusted to her that the Church should do all in her power to remove obstacles to conversion and, positively, to offer inducements to attract those who are in infidelity to embrace the faith of Christ. Pope John XXII, in a Decretal letter given in the year 1320,[3] pointed out that the lot of those who were converted from Judaism should certainly not be worse after baptism than it had been before. He strictly forbade, therefore, that they should be deprived of their temporal possessions; he commanded, rather, that all kindness be shown them to encourage conversion and to prevent subsequent defection.

[1] *Probe te*, 15 dec. 1751, ad 27—*Fontes*, n. 418; cf. Dalpiaz, "Annotationes ad Decretum Sancti Officii,"—*Apollinaris*, X (1937), 335.

[2] *Ius Canonicum ad Codicis Normam Exactum* (7 toms. in 8 vols., Romae: apud Aedes Universitatis Gregorianae, 1923-1938), Vol. V, *Ius Matrimoniale*, n. 631, nota 61. Hereafter cited *Ius Matrimoniale*.

[3] C. 2, *de Iudaeis*, V, 2, in Extravag. com. 2.

Paul III, in the constitution *Cupientes,*[4] given March 21, 1542, stated explicitly that, since the great aim of his pontificate was the conversion of the Jews and of all infidels, he would do all in his power to remove obstacles to their conversion. He then, "*motu proprio et ex certa scientia nostra, auctoritate apostolica,*" decreed that, since many Jews were detained by the fear of temporal loss from becoming Christians, in the future no such loss was to be an obstacle to their conversion. Their goods were to be left intact. If such goods were obtained by usury or dishonest business practices, restitution had to be made to those to whom it was due, provided that such persons were certainly known; if they were not certainly known, or if they had since died, these goods were to be retained by the convert. For the Pope, "*in favorem suscepti Baptismatis,*" determined that such a retention by the convert served a pious cause. Paul III also provided that such converts were not to be disinherited by their parents or relatives, and granted them exemption from certain civil disabilities then affecting Jews.

Clement XI, in his Constitution *Propagandae per Universum,* March 11, 1704,[5] recalled, renewed and even extended the provisions of Paul III in favor of Jewish converts. He, too, mentioned that he, like his predecessors, made this grant by virtue of the apostolic authority given him in favor of the faith, to promote the conversion of infidels.

Benedict XIV could, therefore, scarcely be said to have acted without precedent of any kind. Further, the very principle which he stated clearly and expressly had been invoked implicitly in the past legislation of the Church. It would serve no useful purpose to attempt an exhaustive treatment of every manifestation of this general principle, namely, that in doubtful matters the decision should be made in favor of he faith. The purpose of the following articles will be to demonstrate its existence by a summary consideration of the

[4] *Bullarum Diplomatum et Privilegiorum Sanctorum Romanorum Pontificum Taurinensis Editio* (24 vols. et appendix, Augustae Taurinorum—Neapoli, 1857-1872), VI, 336. Hereafter *Bullarum Romanum.*

[5] *Bullarium Romanum,* XXI, 108.

outstanding instances in which it was employed, instances, indeed, which guided Benedict XIV in the decision set down in his letter *Probe te*.

Article I. The Fourth Council of Toledo

Among the historical references to the general principle that in doubtful matters the decision should always be in favor of the faith, the earliest is in the IV Council of Toledo, held December 5, 633, over which St. Isadore of Seville presided.[6] Canons 59-63 of this Council[7] are the canons which may be considered as embodying implicitly the principle under discussion. They may, therefore, be regarded as a source, indirectly, of the legislation contained in canon 1127 of the Code, or at least as a means which seeks to clarify the application of the same principles as is found there.[8]

Early in the history of the Church in Spain, the large and influential Jewish population constituted at once a grave danger to the faith and an acute problem for the legislation of the Church. The Council of Elvira (306) began to take legislative cognizance of the problem, which in subsequent councils became more and more pressing.[9] The very canons of condemnation indicate plainly the intimacy of the relationships between Christians and Jews.[10]

It is not, of course, to the point to trace here the early history of Spain. Suffice it to say that in the beginning of the fifth century Spain fell under the domination of the Goths, who were Arians. In 587 King Recared (586-601) became a Catholic, and by persuasion rather than force brought his people to the faith with him. In regard to the Jewish problem, his legislation is to be found in the III Council

[6] Hefele-Leclercq, *Histoire des Conciles,* (Nouvelle Traduction Francaise Faite sur La Deuxieme Edition Allemande, 10 vols. in 19, Paris, 1907-1938), tom. III, part I, 266-267.

[7] Mansi, Joannes D., Sacrorum Conciliorum Nova et Amplissima Collectio, (53 vols. in 59, edition edited and printed at Paris, Leipzig, and Arnhem, 1901-1927), X, 633-634. Hereafter quoted as Mansi.

[8] Arendt, "Nota circa canonem 1127"—*ETL*, I (1924), 175; Cappello, *De Sacramentis,* III, n. 788.

[9] Mansi, II, 8; cf. Dale, *The Synod of Elvira* (London, 1882), pp. 254-262.

[10] Canons 16, 49, 50—Mansi, II, 8.

of Toledo (589), canon 14 of which is the only one even remotely connected with the present discussion. It provided that Jews were ineligible for any office that might give them power of punishment over Christians; that if a Christian slave were circumcised he was to be freed and restored to the Catholic religion; that Jews could not have Christian wives and that the children of such unions were to be baptized.[11] King Sisebut (612-621) kept these laws and went even further. Acting independently of the Church, he imposed on his Jewish subjects the choice of compulsory conversion or of exile.[12]

Without this background the canons of the IV Council of Toledo (633) would be unintelligible either in their bearing on the present question or in their influence on the later general legislation of the Church. Canon 58 of this Council clearly implied (what is characteristic of most anti-Jewish legislation) that the former laws had not been enforced. An indication is found here that the Jews had used their wealth to escape the rigor of the laws against them, for this canon established the penalty of excommunication for clerics or laymen who took bribes in return for protection. The Council then proceded to lay down a detailed plan for dealing with the Jews. Canon 57 [13] decreed that, while compulsory conversion was no longer to be practiced, nevertheless those who by violence or by necessity had become Christians were under no circumstances to be allowed to return to Judaism, lest thus the name of God be blasphemed and the Catholic faith be made to appear cheap and contemptible. If such converts dared to have their sons or their slaves circumcised, their sons were to be taken from them and the slaves were to be freed.[14] The text of canon 60 of the Council introduces a difficulty of interpretation. This text, as given by Mansi,[15] demanded that the sons and daughters of Jews were to be separated from their parents in order that they might be brought up under Catholic auspices. In view of the context of the canon and the authority of other manu-

[11] Mansi, IX, 996.

[12] Ziegler, *Church and State in Visigothic Spain* (Washington, D. C.: The Catholic University of America, 1930), pp. 189-196.

[13] Mansi, X, 633.

[14] Canon 59—Mansi, X, 633.

[15] X, 634.

scripts, it seems more logical to restrict the application of this canon to those children who had been baptized.[16] Christian children of apostate Jews were not to be deprived of their inheritance, even though their parents were to be punished by the confiscation of their goods. [17] Nor were baptized Jews to be allowed to associate with the unbaptized members of their race because of the danger of perversion.[18] A Jew was forbidden to live with a Christian wife unless he, too, became a Catholic; children who had been born of the union of a Christian with a Jew were to be brought up in the Catholic religion.[19]

This is the substance of canons 58-63 of the IV Council of Toledo (633). The reason that they are quoted as sources for the principle that in doubtful matters judgment is to be passed in favor of the faith seems to be this: in a conflict between the natural right of parents over their children and the right of the Church acquired by baptism to safeguard the salvation of her subjects, the Fathers of the Council solved the doubt by applying, at least by implication, the principle that the higher right absorbed the lesser. The same is to be said of the law established in canon 63 in regard to the separation of husband and wife, one of the other restrictions placed upon the Jews. It was, therefore, an application of the privilege of the faith taken in its widest, most general sense. It implied the right to choose, in doubtful matters, that probable solution which favored the acquisition or the preservation of the true faith.[20]

Article II—The Privilege of the Faith in the Decretals

The next instance to be considered, in which the privilege of the faith and the favor due to the faith were the determining factors in the solution of doubts, is taken from the Decretals of Gregory IX

[16] Cf. Hefele-Leclercq, *Historie des Conciles*, III, 1, p. 274, note 1.

[17] Canon 61—Mansi, X, 634.

[18] Canon 62—Mansi, X, 634.

[19] Canon 63—Mansi, 634.

[20] Cappello, *De Sacramentis*, III, n. 788; Creusen, "Baptême Douteux et Mariage Indissoluble,"—*NRT*, LII (1925), 229; Léry, *Le Privilège de la Foi*, n. 1.

(1234). It is possible to trace the pertinent canons of the IV Council of Toledo (633) through various Spanish and French canonical collections; through the *Decretum* of Burchard of Worms (+1025);[21] through the collections of Ivo of Chartres (+1117)[22] into the Decree of Gratian (C. 1140).[23] But to do so adds no new development, gives no further light on the question but, on the contrary, serves to promote confusion. There is no evidence that Gregory IX adverted to this conciliar legislation when similar problems came to him for solution, and in the Decree of Gratian, as is evident from the references already noted, the canons are quoted in support of various phases of canonical legislation which are foreign to the subject under discussion.

In a Decretal letter written at Perugia May 27, 1229,[24] and addressed by Gregory IX to Berthold I, Bishop of Strasbourg (1223-1244), a problem somewhat similar to those considered by the IV Council of Toledo received careful consideration and definitive solution. From the text of the letter it is clear that the question presented to Gregory IX for solution had first been brought up at a synod over which Berthold had presided. A certain Jew had been converted to the faith. His wife remained in Judaism. Thereupon the convert demanded that his four year old son be given into his charge to be brought up in the true faith. The mother, however, objected strenuously to this arrangement, claiming that the child needed the care of the mother more than that of the father. Gregory, however, asserting that the child legally was under the care of the father, assigned the boy to him. The principal reason for this decision was the danger that the mother's influence might lead the child into error were he to be left in her care. Gregory, therefore, basing his answer on the principle that the favor of the faith demanded this solution of the doubt proposed, gave the child to the father's care:

[21] Liber IV, cc. 82-86—Migne, Jacques Paul, Patrologiae Curus Completus, Series Latina, (221 vols., Parisiis, 1844-1864), CXL, 742. Hereafter *MPL*.

[22] Decretum, pars I, cc. 276-280—*MPL*, CLXI, 124.

[23] Canon 59 (IV Toledo) in C. 94, D. IV, *de cans;* canon 60 (IV Toledo) in C. 11, C. XXVIII, q. 1.; canon 61 (IV Toledo) in C. 12, C. XXVIII, q. 1.; canon 62 (IV Toledo) in C. 10, C. XXVIII, q. 1.; canon 63 (IV Toledo) in C. 24, C. II, q. 7.

[24] C. 2, X, *de conversione infidelium*, III, 33.

in favorem maxime fidei Christianae respondemus patri eundem puerum assignandum.[25]

The comments of the Decretalists extended this ruling of Pope Gregory IX to the case wherein the mother was the convert. They also pointed out that the civil law, which gave the children to the father's care after their third year, yielded to the favor of the faith, that is, the children were to be given to the care of the Catholic parent. They were to be baptized upon the conversion of the parent if they had not yet reached the age of reason. If there was any doubt whether or not they had reached the age of reason, the favor of the faith demanded that they be placed in the care of the Catholic party.[26]

Article III—The Privilege of the Faith in the Letters of Benedict XIV

To bridge the gap from Gregory IX (1227-1241) to Benedict XIV (1740-1758) it would be necessary to follow the discussions of the classic theologians on the validity, the lawfulness and the consequences of baptism conferred on the children of infidels. This would consume more time and space than its contribution to the final purpose of this study would warrant, namely, the purpose to establish the existence of a general principle by which doubtful matters were to be resolved in favor of the faith.

In two letters [27] Benedict XIV introduced whatever was useful and

[25] C. 2, X, *de conversione infidelium*, III, 33.

[26] Panormitanus (Nicholaus de Tudeschis), *Commentaria in Quinque Libros Decretalium* (5 vols. in 7, Venetiis, 1588), c. 2, X, *de conversione infidelium*, III, 33; Hostiensis (Henricus de Segusio), *Commentaria in Quinque Libros Decretalium* (5 vols. in 3, Venetiis, 1581), lib. II, c. 2, X, *de conversione infidelium*, III, 33; Barbosa, *Collectanea Doctorum tam Veterum quam Recentiorum in Ius Pontificium Universum* (5 vols. in 4, Lugduni, 1656), Vol. II, c. 2, X, *de conversione infidelium*, III, 33; Sanchez, *De Sancto Matrimonii Sacramento Disputationum Libri Decem in Tres Tomos Distributi* (Venetiis, 1712), lib. VII, disp. 73, n. 16; Reiffenstuel, *Ius Canonicum Universum* (5 vols. in 7, Parisiis, 1864-1882), Vol. V, c. 2, X, *de conversione infidelium*, III, 33; Schmalzgrueber, *Ius Canonicum Universum* (5 vols. in 12, Romae, 1843-1845), tom. III, pars 3, *de conversione infidelium*.

[27] *Postremo mense*, 28 febr. 1747—*Fontes*, n. 377; *Probe te*, 15 dec. 1751—*Fontes*, n. 418.

necessary, from such theologians as St. Thomas Aquinas (+1274), Scotus (+1308) and Durandus (+1334) to establish this principle. For in these letters Benedict proposed to settle definitively the extent of the Church's rights in relation to the baptism of infidels. Following the teaching of St. Thomas, Benedict XIV decided that baptism administered to a child, despite the fact that the infidel parents were unwilling, was nevertheless valid. The opinion of Durandus,[28] denying the validity of the baptism so conferred, he rejected as being singular and without theological foundation.[29] He agreed also with the opinion of St. Thomas (1225-1274) [30] that such a procedure was wrong and that such an administration of baptism was illicit. While he did not openly condemn Scotus' opinion that Catholic princes and kings could lawfully force their infidel subjects to be baptized, he showed that, because of the inherent dangers of such practices, he agreed rather with St. Thomas, who opposed this view as being against the tradition of the Church.[31] Therefore, even the apparent good derivable from the propagation of the faith did not justify the baptism of infidel children whose parents objected. This was rather a means to injure than to favor the faith; such baptism was conferred licitly only in the case of danger of death, or when the parents had abandoned the child, or when the parents had lost their rights over the child.[32]

But if, despite the unlawfulness of the act, children had been baptized, then the rights of the parents conflicted with the rights of the Church, and the doubt was to be settled in favor of the faith. The child was to be taken from the infidel parents in order to ensure its education in the Catholic faith by Christians.[33] This rule, of

[28] *In Petri Lombardi Sententias Theologicas Commentariorum Libri Quattuor* (Venetiis, 1586), Dist. IV, q. VII, a. 13.

[29] *Postremo mense*, ad 26-27—*Fontes*, n. 377. Cf. decisions of the Holy Office cited there.

[30] *Summa Theologica*, IIa IIae, q. X, a. 12; IIIa. q. LXVIII, a. 10; *Quodlibetales*, II, a. 7.

[31] *Postremo mense*, ad 4-5—*Fontes*, n. 377; *Probe te*, ad 10—Fontes, n. 418.

[32] *Postremo mense*, ad 8; *Probe te*, ad 14-15.

[33] *Postremo mense*, ad 29-30.

course, now stands modified by the doctrine of the modern theologians. The general harm such a course would cause today would outbalance the favor shown to the faith in an individual case. But it must be remembered that the rule as enacted during the pontificate of Benedict XIV constituted legislation for the Papal States, the population of which was not only predominantly but almost universally Catholic.

A doubt also arose from the fact that the conversion of only one of the infidel parents could occasion domestic disputes when the convert insisted on the baptism of the children. Benedict XIV resolved this doubt in favor of the converted parent. If the father was the convert, both natural and civil law recognized his right to insist on the baptism of his children, even though the mother objected.[34]

The rights of the mother, when she was the convert, had been considered by Benedict in section sixteen of the letter *Postremo mense* in a rather cursory fashion. But they were subjected to a thorough examination in the subsequent letter *Probe te.* Benedict XIV decided that the mother had a right, founded in natural law, to have a part in the education of her children. If the father opposed her wish to have the children baptized, there was a conflict of rights. Gregory IX [35] had already laid the foundation for the solution: in doubtful matters the decision must be in favor of the faith.[36] Hence the child was to be baptized.

Benedict XIV extended the right of offering a child for baptism even to the grandmother, despite the opposition of the child's Jewish mother and guardians. The grandparents, even according to civil law, had some share in the power of the parents over the child.[37] Thus the grandmother had at least a doubtful right, and in such a conflict of rights the decision was to turn in favor of the faith.

It was Benedict XIV who, for the first time, insistently framed a clear expression of the general privilege of the faith which the

[34] *Postremo mense*, ad 15; *Probe te*, ad 11; cf. c. 2, X, *de conversione infidelium*, III, 33.

[35] C. 2, X, *de conversione infidelium*, III, 33.

[36] *Probe te*, ad 18, 19, 25, 26—*Fontes*, n. 418.

[37] *Postremo mense*, ad 17—*Fontes*, n. 377; *Probe te*, ad 1, 12, 22, 25—*Fontes*, n. 418.

present chapter, and particularly the specific study of Benedict's letters, intended to demonstrate. According to the doctrine of Benedict it was the obligation of the Pope to promote the faith to the highest extent of his abilities, in so far as he could do this without injury to the strict rights of others.[38] He based his decisions of the doubts proposed to him in these letters on the general principle, which is also the ultimate basis of canon 1127: "*In re dubia in favorem fidei pronuntiandum esse, constans regula est.*" [39]

[38] *Probe te,* 15 dec. 1751, ad 26—*Fontes,* n. 418.
[39] *Probe te,* 15 dec. 1751, ad 27—*Fontes,* n. 418.

Chapter III

THE PRIVILEGE OF THE FAITH AND INFIDEL MARRIAGE

The general principle that in doubtful matters it is a constant rule of ecclesiastical jurisprudence to pronounce in favor of the faith is, evidently, one which receives its specification from the nature of the doubt which evokes its application. Canon 1127 furnishes the most important of these determining agencies. In this canon the term "privilege of the faith," from its position within the article "*De Dissolutione Vinculi,*" refers to the Pauline Privilege and to all other cases in which the bond of legitimate marriage is dissolved in favor of the faith. When there is present an insoluble doubt about the verification of the conditions necessary for the application of the Pauline Privilege, or of the Constitutions of canon 1125, these doubts are to be resolved in favor of the faith, for the privilege of the faith enjoys the favor of the law.

Though the Pauline Privilege is almost as old as the Church, the principle of canon 1127 has a much more recent appearance. Its earliest manifestation is found only in the sixteenth century, and its fuller development only in the jurisprudence of the Roman Curia during the eighteenth and nineteenth centuries. Therefore, to understand the legislation contained in canon 1127, it is first necessary to understand the conditions which need certainly to be realized for the application of the Pauline Privilege. For when these conditions are only doubtfully realized, or when they are certainly not realized, then recourse must be had to the wider Privilege of the Faith, that is to say, to the power of the Pope over marriages contracted and even consummated in infidelity, for as this power is applied through canon 1125, so it is implied through canon 1127.

Article I. The Pauline Privilege

A. *Foundation and Development of Necessary Conditions*

In St. Paul's First Epistle to the Corinthians [1] there is found the

[1] I Cor., VII: 12-16.

basis for the privilege which bears his name.

> "For the rest I speak, not the Lord: If any brother hath a wife that believeth not, and she consent to dwell with him, let him not put her away. And if any woman hath a husband that believeth not and he consent to dwell with her, let her not put away her husband. For the unbelieving husband is sanctified by the believing wife; and the unbelieving wife is sanctified by the believing husband: otherwise your children should be unclean; but now they are holy. But if the unbeliever depart let him depart. For a brother or sister is not under servitude in such cases. But God hath called us in peace. For how knowest thou, O wife, whether thou shalt save thy husband? Or how knowest thou, O man, whether thou shalt save thy wife?"

The limits of the Pauline Privilege are laid down in this passage, but the text is not without difficulties. In the writings of the Fathers, in the statements of the Holy See, in the writings of theologians and canonists, there is a gradual clarification of the privilege and a solution of the more difficult problems of its application. From verses 12-16 of the seventh chapter of I Corinthians it is evident that St. Paul was speaking to those who were parties of a mixed union because of the conversion of one spouse.[2] St. Paul himself indicated clearly that he regarded marriages entered into in infidelity as true and valid unions, for he approved the continuance of these marriages wherever it was possible, even after conversion. And this, of course, has also been the view of the Church. She has regarded these marriages as indissoluble, except in so far as God has given the power of dissolution to His Church for the salvation of souls.[3]

St. Paul, therefore, in consequence of a power divinely conceded to him, established this privilege in virtue of which a marriage validly

[2] Cornelius a Lapide, *Commentarius in Omnes Divi Pauli Epistolas* (2. ed., Hieronymus Albritius, Venetiis, 1717), p. 193; Gigot, *Christ's Teaching Concerning Divorce in the New Testament* (New York, 1912), p. 134.

[3] Pius IX, *Syllabus*, prop. 67—H. Denzinger—C. Bannwart, *Enchiridion Symbolorum, Definitionum et Declarationum de Rebus Fidei et Morum* (17. ed., Friburgi Brisgoviae: Herder, 1928), n. 1767; Wernz, *Ius Decretalium*, (6 vols. in 8, Prati, 1908-1915), Vol. IV *Ius Matrimoniale*, nn. 30, 696. Hereafter *Ius Matrimoniale*.

contracted and consummated in infidelity could be dissolved if one of the parties was baptized and the one remaining in infidelity departed.[4] The privilege, of course, accorded to the convert the right to enter a new marriage.[5] St. Paul did not intend this privilege to be used by those who married after one of the contracting parties had already been baptized. For in that case those whose marriages had proved unhappy could have used the privilege to the abuse rather than the favor of the faith.[6]

The Church has always understood the text as applying to marriages between two infidels, one of whom later became a Catholic. This interpretation was written into thirteenth century canon law when a letter of Innocent III (1198-1216) so stating the privilege was placed in the Decretals.[7] Pope Celestine III (1191-1198) seemed to think that if the husband in a Christian marriage apostatized and abandoned his wife to marry a pagan, the wife should be free to enter a second valid union.[8] This appears to have been a speculative answer to a theoretical rather than to an actual case. At any rate, Innocent III expressed the correct doctrine.[9] Hence the Pauline Privilege applies only to a *valid marriage* contracted in *infidelity*.

B. *The Departure of the Unconverted Spouse*

St. Paul's words, "If the unbeliever depart, let him depart," are not specific, and consequently there has been much speculation as to the interpretation of them. This interpretation was left to the Church

[4] Vermeersch, *De Casu Apostoli*, n. 2.

[5] Sanchez, *De Matrimonio*, lib. VII, disp. LXXIV, n. 4; Perrone, *Praelectiones Theologicae* (32. ed., Taurini, 1868), I, *Tractatus de Matrimonio*, c. II, prop. II, p. 432; Gregory, *The Pauline Privilege* (The Catholic University of America Canon Law Studies, n. 68, Washington, D. C.: The Catholic University of America, 1931), p. 76.

[6] Cappello, *De Sacramentis*, III, *De Matrimonio*, n. 789. Cf. S.C.S. Off., resp. (Cochinchin), 1 aug. 1759, ad 4—*Fontes*, n. 810; S.C.S. Off., resp. (Nankin), 5 mart. 1852—*Fontes*, n. 918.

[7] Ep. *Quanto te magis*—c. 7, X, *de divortiis*, IV, 19.

[8] Ep. *Laudabilem*—c. 1, X, *de conversione infidelium*, III, 33; the part of the letter expressing this opinion is omitted.

[9] *Quanto te magis*—c. 7, X, *de divortiis*, IV, 19; Gregory, *The Pauline Privilege*, p. 31, note 94; pp. 32, 33.

to be determined as need arose. The departure, of course, was essential to the use of the privilege. In the course of time it became increasingly necessary to know whether this departure exclusively meant an actual, physical abandonment of the convert, or whether the actions of the infidel, when these were highly dangerous to the faith or morals of the convert, or when they involved grave insults to God and to the faith, could be taken as moral, culpable departure on the part of the infidel.

The original Greek, according to some authorities, should be translated not "If the unbeliever depart, let him depart," but: "If the unbeliever is the cause of separation, let him cause separation." [10] In this sense St. Paul would not have limited the use of the privilege to those converts whose spouses actually departed by refusing cohabitation. It would apply to those whose infidel spouses made peaceful cohabitation impossible because of their insults to the Catholic religion and because of their attempts to lead the convert into sin.

St. John Chrysostom (C. 344-407) so understood this condition of the privilege in his 19th Homily on I Corinthians.[11] Inquiring into the meaning of the words: "If the unbeliever depart," he answered that if the Christian spouse was ordered to offer sacrifice, or to be the infidel's partner in impiety because of the marriage, it was better that the marriage bond be broken than that the convert be led to the commission of grave sin. And if the infidel constantly caused strife on this account, he was the cause of the separation. Indeed, from the very force of the words he used, St. John Chrysostom showed clearly that he recognized in such circumstances the convert's right to remarry.[12]

Such also is the testimony of the *Commentaria in Tredecim Epistolas Beati Pauli,* written about 370, and for centuries mistakenly attributed to St. Ambrose. The commentary is known now as the

[10] Joyce, *Christian Marriage* (London and New York: Sheed and Ward, 1932), p. 483; cf. Burton, *A Commentary on Canon 1125.* The Catholic University of America Canon Law Studies, n. 121, Washington, D. C.: The Catholic University of America Press, 1940), pp. 6-7.

[11] Migne, *Patrologiae Cursus Completus, Series Graeca,* (161 vols., Parisiis, 1856-1866), LXI, 155. Hereafter MPG.

[12] Léry, *Le Privilège de la Foi,* n. 11.

"Ambrosiaster." [13] This anonymous author in unmistakable language declared that the Pauline Privilege could effect a complete dissolution of the marriage bond and correspondingly grant the right to a new marriage. With equal clearness he also specified the condition for the application of the privilege now under discussion, for he said: "*Sed si infidelis odio Dei discedit, fidelis non erit reus dissoluti matrimonii . . . Contumelia enim Creatoris solvit ius matrimonii circa eum qui relinquitur.*" [14] Thus it became clear that the departure of the infidel gave rise to the right of remarriage for the convert by giving grounds for the complete severance of the marriage bond.

C. *The Time of Dissolution*

When it became clear that the Pauline Privilege gave the convert the right to enter a new marriage, canonists and theologians turned their attention to the determination of the precise time when the bond of the former marriage was dissolved. Hostiensis (+1271) and those who agreed with him,[15] basing their opinion on a false interpretation of "Ambrosiaster's" principle: "*Contumelia Creatoris solvit ius matrimonii circa eum qui relinquitur,*" taught that the bond was dissolved by the infidel's departure. They consequently denied that the second valid marriage was the efficient cause of the dissolution.

But the opinion that the former bond was dissolved by the second marriage—the much more common opinion—was the one that prevailed. The strongest argument in favor of this opinion was a decision of Innocent III in his letter *Gaudemus*. Innocent ruled that a convert who had separated from his infidel spouse had to return to her if her conversion preceded his prospective exercise of the right to remarry.[16] Evidently it was Innocent's opinion that the bond of the former marriage endured until it was dissolved by the subsequent

[13] For a full discussion of this question, consult Gregory, *The Pauline Privilege*, p. 17, Léry, *Le Privilège de la Foi*, n. 12; Burton, *A Commentary on Canon 1125*, p. 7.

[14] *MPL*, XVII, 231; cf. c. 2, C. XXVIII, q. 2.

[15] Cf. Pontius, *De Sacramento Matrimonii Tractatus* (2. ed. Bruxellis, 1627), lib. IX, c. 4, n. 16.

[16] C. 8, X, *de divortiis*, IV, 19.

marriage. St. Thomas agreed with this conclusion and attributed the dissolution to the stronger bond of sacramental marriage which loosened the former and weaker bond of the marriage contracted in infidelity.[17]

D. *The Necessity of the Interpellations*

From the terms of its concession, the Pauline Privilege demands that the infidel be the cause of the separation. The departure of the infidel is, therefore, not to be presumed; it must be proved. This proof generally is to be obtained through the interpellations which afford the infidel an opportunity to manifest his intentions in regard to conversion or peaceful cohabitation. Some form of interpellation must have been required implicitly by all the legislation in regard to the Pauline Privilege. There is evidence from the time of St. Augustine that it was necessary to determine the intentions of the infidel. Innocent III referred indirectly to interpellations in two of his letters.[18] In them he determined that the infidel was to be considered as departing if at all he refused cohabitation, or if he consented to cohabitation but not without blasphemy of the Divine name, or not without attempting to draw the convert into mortal sin.

Canon 63 of the IV Council of Toledo (633), which Santi considered as the first legislation requiring the interpellations,[19] gave rise to a dispute as to whether the convert was free to remarry if the infidel was willing to cohabit peacefully, but if at the same time the latter was unwilling to be converted. For the Council ruled that a convert from Judaism could not remain with a spouse who remained in Judaism; conversion was required.[20]

Through its inclusion in the Decree of Gratian, this canon exercised a considerable influence on canonical thought. But its prescrip-

[17] IV Sent., dist. XXXIX, q. un., art. 5, ad 1, 2. Cf. Sanchez, *De Matrimonio*, lib. VII, disp. LXXV, n. 4; Arendt, "Nota circa canonem 1127"—*ETL*, I (1924), 174.

[18] Cc. 7, 8, *de divortiis*, IV, 19; Wernz, *Ius Matrimoniale*, n. 702, nota 72.

[19] Santi, *Praelectiones Iuris Canonici* (2 vols., Ratisbon, 1886), II, p. 174, n. 10.

[20] C. 63—Mansi, X, 634.

tion had no more than local value; it was legislation demanded by particular circumstances of time and place. The mind of the Church was to be found in a decretal of Clement III (1187-1191), written in the year 1188. Clement ruled that if the wife of a convert Jew or Saracen did not wish to be converted but was willing to cohabit peacefully, the convert could not use the Pauline Privilege.[21] It is only after the Council of Trent, when the privilege became of great practical importance, that the legislation assumed more definite form. A response of the Sacred Congregation of the Council, January 23, 1603, promulgated the first clear and unambiguous legislation on this requirement.[22] According to this decree the infidel had to be asked if he was willing to accept Christianity and if he would live peacefully without insult to God.

This brief consideration of the essential elements of the Pauline Privilege in the light of their historical development is, from two viewpoints, necessary to an understanding of the principle of canon 1127. It was in regard to the fulfillment of these conditions that many doubts could arise. And, from this consideration, it is clear that the principle, "in doubtful matters the privilege of the faith enjoys the favor of the law," was not invoked in the Pre-Tridentine development of the Pauline Privilege. In the early days of the Church there was almost a complete silence about the privilege.[23] The later canonists and theologians were concerned with the determination of the strict requirement of the privilege. It is not surprising, therefore, that the supplementary principle applicable in doubtful cases was not mentioned. It is only during the great period of mission activities, beginning in the sixteenth century, that the principle here being considered found application.

[21] C. 1, *de conversione infidelium*, III, 20, in Compil. II.

[22] Cf. *De Synodo Dioecesana*, lib. XIII, c. 21, n. 1; cf. Feije, *De Impedimentis et Dispensationibus Matrimonialibus* (3. ed., Lovanii, 1885), n. 475; S.C. de Prop. de Fide (ad C.P. pro Sin.), 16 iunii 1697—*Collectanea S. Congregationis de Propaganda Fide* (2 vols., Romae, 1907), n. 634. Hereafter *Coll. S.C.P.F.*

[23] Arendt, "La tradizione cattolica in favore del Privilegio Paolino nel coniuge infedele batezzato in una setta acattolica,"—*Gregorianum*, IV (1923), 258; Wernz-Vidal, *Ius Matrimoniale*, n. 631, nota 57; Joyce, *Christian Marriage*, pp. 469 and 473.

ARTICLE II. THE CONSTITUTIONS OF PAUL III, ST. PIUS V AND GREGORY XIII

The sixteenth century explorations of the Spanish and the Portuguese in the East and in the West had opened up vast territories for missionary activity. The matrimonial problems which those charged with these missions encountered either clearly could not be solved by the application of the Pauline Privilege, or the marriage resulting upon its application remained of doubtful validity. For by the Pauline Privilege a convert whose infidel spouse upon being interpellated either was unwilling to be converted or refused to cohabit peacefully acquired the right to enter a second marriage. Where polygamy was not the custom of the infidels, the verification of the necessary conditions was not difficult. Where, as was the custom among the tribes of the New World, polygamy was the rule, the difficulties of the missionaries in solving the marriage problems of catechumens can easily be imagined.

It was difficult to know what was to be done for a man who had had many wives simultaneously or even successively, but who could not remember which of them he had taken first. The validity of the first marriage or of any of the other unions could be questioned, and the problem often defied solution. It was to give an authoritative answer to such problems that Paul III and St. Pius V issued their constitutions. Although authors do not generally consider these constitutions as applications of the principle that the judgment in doubtful matters should be in favor of the faith, nevertheless the whole tone of the discussion of those who have studied them forces one to the conclusion that it is here that the foundations for the principle of canon 1127 were laid.[24]

Such is he opinion of Dalpiaz.[25] As he points out, although the constitutions do not necessarily treat of doubtful cases, they do show that the principle enunciated by Benedict XIV was here implicitly

[24] Cf. Burton, *A Commentary on Canon 1125*, pp. 25-29; 30-35; Woods, *The Constitutions of Canon 1125* (Milwaukee: Bruce, 1935), p. 45; pp. 53, 54.

[25] "Annotationes ad Decretum Sancti Officii, die 10a iunii 1937"—*Apollinaris*, X (1937), 386.

invoked and applied in regard to marriage problems. Of the same opinion, apparently, was Wernz.[26] For, in attempting to determine the juridical basis of certain responses of the Holy Office, in which the principle that in doubtful cases the judgment should be in favor of the faith was employed, Wernz adverted to the constitutions of Paul III and St. Pius V as further evidence of the application of the same principle. A consideration of the dispositions of these constitutions supports such a conclusion.

A. *The Constitution* ALTITUDO *of Paul III*

In his Constitution *Altitudo*[27] Paul III established the following legislation for concerted polygamous infidels:

> "Super eorum vero matrimoniis hoc observandum decernimus, ut qui ante conversionem plures iuxta eorum mores habebant uxores, et non recordantur quam primo acceperint, conversi ad fidem unam ex illis accipiant quam voluerint, ut cum ea matrimonium contrahant per verba de praesenti, ut moris est; qui vero recordantur quam primo acceperint, aliis dimissis, eam retineant. Ac eis concedimus ut coniuncti etiam in tertio gradu tam consanguinitatis quam affinitatis non excluduntur a matrimoniis contrahendis donec huic S. Sedi super hoc aliud visum fuerit statuendum."

The concessions in regard to consanguinity and affinity are not of immediate importance here. The point is that if a polygamist did not remember who his first wife was, then because of his ignorance none of his so-called marriages could be considered as of more than doubtful value.[28]

Paul III, then, really applied the principle that these doubtful cases should be solved in favor of the faith. Certainly he did not regard all of the marriages of infidel polygamists, even the first, as invalid.

[26] *Ius Matrimoniale*, n. 701, nota 66; cf. Wernz-Vidal, *Ius Matrimoniale*, n. 631, nota 61.

[27] 1 iunii 1537—Docum. VI, C.I.C.

[28] Vermeersch, *De Casu Apostoli*, n. 81, p. 5; Payen, *De Matrimonio in Missionibus ac Potissimum in Sinis* (3 vols. 2. ed., Zi-ka-wei: in Typographia T'ou-sè-wè, 1936), n. 2405.

The constitution would not have granted any favor in allowing remarriage to an infidel who had never been validly married. But it is equally certain that he regarded as doubtful the marriages of those who could not remember who were their first wives. Therefore, to solve these doubtful cases and to facilitate thereby conversion to the faith by the fulness of pontifical power, he dissolved the bond of marriage validly contracted in infidelity if such a bond existed, and allowed the convert to marry the one of his so-called wives whom he preferred, by means of the exchange of matrimonial consent. Modern commentators say in so many words that when there is no impediment of consanguinity, the Constitution *Altitudo* grants nothing that is not granted by canon 1127.[29] But canon 1127 states the principle that in doubtful matters the privilege of the faith enjoys the favor of the law. The conclusion, therefore, is that in regard to infidels who do not remember the identity of their first wives, Paul III applied the same principle.

B. *The Constitution* ROMANI PONTIFICIS *of St. Pius V*

That the concession granted by Paul III failed to solve all the difficulties encountered by missionaries is evident. For in his Constitution *Romani Pontificis,* August 2, 1571, St. Pius V granted a wider privilege. Paul III had decreed that converts who in infidelity had had many wives and who could not remember who had been the first and legitimate wife could choose any one of them and contract a valid marriage with her. One practical difficulty soon suggested itself. Some of the Indians for whom the privilege had been granted, having been granted one wife under the conditions mentioned, declared that another had been the first.[30] Such a consideration could very possibly have been one of the motives which moved St. Pius V to widen the concession of Paul III, for this would have been a source of grave scruples to the missionaries. His legislation was as follows:

> " . . . Cum itaque, sicut accepimus, Indis in sua infidelitate manentibus plures permittantur uxores, quas ipsi etiam

[29] De Smet, *Tractatus Theologico-Canonicus de Sponsalibus et Matrimonio,* 4 ed. (Brugis; Beyaert, 1927) n. 355, nota 5; Payen, *op. cit.*, n. 2405; Vromant, "Le Privilège de la Foi au Canon 1127"—*NRT*, LIX (1932), 443.

[30] Burton, *A Commentary on Canon 1125*, p. 32, n. 8.

levissimis de causis repudiant, hinc factum est quod recipientibus baptismum, permissum sit permanere cum ea uxore, quae simul cum marito existit; et quia saepenumero contingit illam non esse primam coniugem, unde tam ministri quam Episcopi gravissimis scrupulis torquentur, existimantes illud non esse verum matrimonium; sed quia durissimum esset separare eos ab uxoribus, cum quibus ipsi Indi baptismum susceperunt, maxime quia difficillimum foret primam coniugem reperire; ideo Nos, statui dictorum Indorum, paterno affectu benigne consulere, atque Ipsos Episcopos et ministros ab huiusmodi scrupulis eximere volentes, motu proprio et ex certa scientia Nostra, ac apostolicae potestatis plenitudine, ut Indi, sic ut praemittitur baptizati, et in futurum baptizandi, cum uxore, quae cum ipsis, baptizata et baptizabitur, remanere valeant cum uxore legitima, aliis dimissis, apostolica auctoritate, tenore praesentium, declaramus, matrimoniumque huiusmodi inter eos legitime consistere . . . "[31]

This constitution was meant, therefore, for those who could be included under the term *Indi*. As is apparent, St. Pius V was well informed of the difficulties in the mission field. The pagan Indians were permitted many wives whom they repudiated for the slightest reasons. Upon conversion they had been permitted to remain with the wife who was baptized with them. But because this wife was not the first wife, the missionaries had become scrupulous for fear that such were not true marriages but adulterous unions. It would seem that in the cases here contemplated, as in the constitution of Paul III, the first wife was unknown. Otherwise, by means of the interpellations and the use of the Pauline Privilege, there would have been no grounds for scruples. It is not to be presumed that the interpellations were being omitted without grave reason.

As a matter of fact, the words of St. Pius V, "*Maxima quia difficillimum foret primum coniugem reperire,*" lend themselves readily to such an interpretation and were in fact so interpreted by the Holy Office.[32] So interpreted, they would represent the application of the same principle that characterized the disposition of Paul III.

[31] Docum. VII, C.*I*.C.

[32] S.C.S. Off. (Siam), 22 nov. 1871—*Coll. S.C.P.F.*, n. 1377; Payen, *De Matrimonio in Missionibus*, n. 2407.

The marriage in question would be doubtful because the identity of the first wife was unknown or at least doubtful, and Pius V, in favor of the faith, would be dissolving the bond of the first marriage if such a bond really existed. If the first marriage was really valid in the case wherein the first wife was certainly known and recognized as such, then the constitution had the force of dissolving a certainly valid marriage in favor of the faith. That, of course, was a greater concession than that of dissolving a bond which was only doubtful. And, as has already been indicated, the marriages of polygamist infidels who took several wives at one time were in many cases doubtful in character. Accordingly one is not reading a wishful sense into the constitution of St. Pius V if one sees in it also, at least by implication, an application of the principle in question—that in doubtful cases the judgment should be in favor of the faith.

C. *The Constitution* POPULIS *of Gregory XIII*

It was intended in the constitutions of Paul III and St. Pius V to solve the problems of polygamist converts. The constitution *Populis* of Gregory XIII, issued January 25, 1585, made no such distinction. It could be used even by a convert from infidelity who had had only one wife. It was occasioned by the African slave trade and the matrimonial problems caused thereby. To reproduce the full text of the constitution here would not be of great benefit; it is of interest in relation to the historical background of canon 1127 only indirectly.[33] Pope Gregory indicated his belief that marriages contracted in infidelity were valid; but he also stated that they were not so firm that, should necessity demand it, they could not be dissolved.

Many of those who were captured and carried into slavery were married persons. Since their marital status was in its consequence a bar to conversion, some solution was highly desirable. Gregory XIII, therefore, granted faculties to the ordinaries and missioners of the countries affected, and to those members of the Society of Jesus who were approved by their superiors to hear confessions, by which faculties they could dispense from the required interpellations, under the

[33] Cf. Docum. VIII, C.I.C.

conditions which as a result of the slave trade, rendered it practically impossible to make them. The convert so dispensed could, after his conversion, marry another Catholic, provided that it was evident from a summary and extrajudicial investigation that the absent spouse could not be interpellated or had not answered the interpellation. The marriage thus contracted was declared to be valid even if it became known later that the former partner had been hindered by a just reason from answering, or that he had been converted at the time his partner entered this second marriage.

From this it is clear that Pope Gregory dissolved the bond of the first marriage, a bond which he considered as true and valid. It offered an *a fortiori* argument that his provision would avail also if the former bond was doubtful. If the certain bond could be dissolved, certainly a doubtful bond could be. This constitution, therefore, is fundamental in demonstrating the ministerial power of the Pope over the bond of legitimate marriage, the use of which power was postulated by the provision that in doubtful cases the judgment should be in favor of the faith.

Thus it became clear that the first application of the principle that in doubtful cases the judgment should be in favor of the faith was made in these constitutions, called into juristic being by the missionary problems of the sixteenth century. The history of the Pauline Privilege up to the time of the Council of Trent (1545-1563) showed no such development. The new problems to be solved led to a more complete knowledge of the powers of the Holy Father as Vicar of Christ. These powers of the Pope over legitimate marriage, as manifested in the constitutions just considered, represented an implicit application of and an evident basis for the principle of canon 1127, for the Pauline Privilege and the constitutions of Paul III, St. Pius V and Gregory XIII reflected the privilege of the faith as it is understood in canon 1127. And, surely, this privilege was recognized as enjoying the favor of the law in doubtful cases.

Article III. A Decision of Urban VIII

Approximately fifty years after the constitution of Pope Gregory XIII matrimonial difficulties in missionary lands were again brought to the Holy See for solution. South America had become a fertile field for converts, and it was from the Jesuit missionaries in the Province of Paraquaria [34] that an appeal was made to Urban VIII (1623-1644). Nicolaus del Techo (1611-1685) was a Jesuit missionary and the historian of the Paraguay mission. In his history [35] he related the difficulties of the mission. The Guarani natives, as pagans, had many concubines and the obligation of Christian monogamy was a great hindrance to their conversion. Some of the missionaries required them, upon conversion, to keep their first wife; others allowed them to choose any of their concubines to be their Christian wives.

Not later than 1634 (for in that year he became a Cardinal), the then Father John de Lugo (1583-1660) laid the problem before Urban VIII. He explained to the Pope that in this mission the natives frequently, when they took a wife, took also her daughters and her sisters, if she had any, and that the wives so taken were dismissed with as little ceremony as Europeans dismissed servants. For this reason many missionaries thought that such unions did not denote true marriage but mere concubinage, and therefore, upon conversion, allowed the natives to keep a baptized partner. Other missionaries, however, became scrupulous over this solution. They required the convert to return to his first wife. Many natives therefore refused conversion; others contended that they had no other wife; and still others pretended to return to the first wife but in reality chose another. Moreover, it was almost impossible for the natives to remember who had been the first wife. Even when she was found, it was necessary to determine whether she had been previously married and whether her husbands had been, in turn, previously married. To complicate matters further, the natives had no external sign by which it was possible to distinguish true matrimonial consent from the sign which they employed when they took a concubine for a brief period.

The reply of Urban VIII is often quoted as a historical source and

[34] Paraquaria was a great mission of the Paraguay district, in the central part of South America between Brazil and Peru.—Nicolaus del Techo, *Historia Provinciae Paraquariae Societatis Jesu* (Leodii, 1673), lib. I, cap. XVI, p. 12.

[35] *Historia Provinciae Paraquariae*, lib. X, cap. XV, pp. 277-278.

confirmation of the principle of canon 1127.[36] For, according to Techo who seems to be the only authority for the statement, Urban replied that the missionaries were authorized to follow whatever opinion proved to be the more favorable one for the converts.

What De Lugo asked, in view of the difficulties he described, was that the missionaries be allowed to dispense the converts so that they could contract a true marriage before the Church. He referred to two briefs of Urban VIII, related by Techo to have been granted October 20, 1626, and September 17, 1627, in which it is said that Urban used the words "*Nos attendentes huiusmodi matrimonia infidelium non ita censeri, quin necessitate suadente dissolvi possint.*" He reminded Urban that the conversion of the infidels provided a sufficiently grave cause for the dissolution of these marriages. The conclusion thus is that De Lugo asked the Pope to intervene in order to solve the very doubtful bond of such marriages in favor of the faith.

Urban, according to this account, replied that he did not see the need of a special dispensation which opinion he evidently based on his conviction that all the marriages were of but very doubtful value.

> "Urbanus Octavus indicto Sapientium virorum super ea re consulto, pronuntiavit non videri sibi speciali sua dispensatione opus esse, sed ubi Doctorum sententiae utrimque probabiles intercederent sequerentur opiniones pro conditione locorum ac hominum Barbaris favorabiliores, salva interim utriusque partis authoritate, sinerent doctis hominibus sentiendi libertatem."

But to be of any value, this response would have to mean that Urban intended to dissolve the doubtful bond if it did exist. A probable opinion is of no value, for if it were that would mean that it is allowable to contract a marriage with a probable impediment of prior bond. St. Alphonsus[37] thought that the Pope allowed such a marriage and that with such authorization it would be permissible

[36] Gasparri, *Tractatus Canonicus de Matrimonio* (Romae, 1904), n. 21; Feije, *De Impedimentis et Dispensationibus Matrimonialibus*, n. 486, nota 4; De Becker, *Praelectiones Canonicae de Matrimonio* (ed. nova ad tramites C.I.C., Louvain: Fr. Ceuterick, 1931), p. 259.

[37] *Theologia Moralis* (4 vols., ed. Gaudè Romae, Typis polyglottis Vaticanis, 1905-1912), VI, n. 972.

to enter marriage with a probable diriment impediment. But a better legal opinion is expressed in *Civiltà Cattolica.*[38] The statement means that the Pope dispenses from the doubtful bond in favor of the faith. In this sense the reply of Urban VIII is indeed a clear expression of the principle that in doubtful matters the judgment should be in favor of the faith.

This reply of Urban VIII is the last evidence of direct intervention on the part of the Popes in such marriage problems. The missionary activity continued and increased. As a result every phase of the Pauline Privilege was subjected to careful study; every form of matrimonial problem was scrutinized by the Roman Congregations to whom these matters were committed by the Holy Father and through whom he exercised his powers. It remains now to trace the historical background of the principle of canon 1127 where it found its clearest and most unequivocal application and development—in the jurisprudence of the Roman Curia; in the decrees of the Sacred Congregation of the Council; in the decrees of the Congregation for the Propagation of the Faith; and especially, in the decrees of the Supreme Congregation of the Holy Office, to whose competence questions relative to the Pauline Privilege and the wider Privilege of the Faith were early committed.

[38] "La Potesta del Papa intorno al Matrimonio degli Infedeli," *Civiltà Cattolica*, series 13, XI (1888), 695.

CHAPTER IV

THE JURISPRUDENCE OF THE ROMAN CURIA

When it had been established in the sixteenth century that the bond of legitimate marriage could be dissolved by the ministerial power of the Pope, the foundation for the principle of canon 1127 was securely laid. In 1751 Benedict XIV enunciated the general principle that in doubtful matters the judgment should be in favor of the faith. The influence of this principle is clearly discernible in a response of the Holy Office, given August 1, 1759.[1]

Benedict had written in reply to a question about the lawfulness of baptizing a child presented by its grandmother despite the opposition of the child's Jewish mother: "*sicut pro primo casu militet Ius Gentium, ita pro altero favor religionis . . .* " In the reply of the Holy Office to a question about the application of the Pauline Privilege in a case where the infidel had departed because of reasons other than hatred of the true faith are the words: "*Cum militet ex parte conversi coniugis favor fidei, eo uti potest qua cumque de causa, dummodo iusta sit.*"

The striking verbal similarity of these passages, and the fact that in its instruction to the Vicar Apostolic of Central Oceania the Holy Office expressly mentions Benedict's statement, substantiate the statement of those who, like Dalpiaz,[2] hold that the Holy Office applied the general principle of Benedict XIV to the matrimonial problems of converts from infidelity. For it is quite apparent that, during the eighteenth and nineteenth centuries, the principle of the favor of the faith in doubtful cases was frequently applied by the Holy Office to solve cases to which the application of the Pauline Privilege was only doubtful. But, before any consideration of the nature of these responses in detail, it will be useful to explore a few notions about the Congregation within whose competence such cases fell.

[1] S.C.S. Off. (Cochinchin.)—*Fontes*, n. 810.

[2] *Apollinaris*, X (1937), 336.

INTRODUCTION: THE SACRED CONGREGATION OF THE HOLY OFFICE

In the seventeenth century, and until the present codification of canon law, three Congregations exercised cumulative jurisdiction in regard to the sacrament of matrimony; the Sacred Congregation of the Holy Office, the Congregation of the Council and the Congregation for the Propagation of the Faith. But almost from its inception the Holy Office alone had jurisdiction in questions pertaining to the Pauline Privilege and the impediment of Disparity of Worship.[3]

The Holy Office was established as a Congregation by Paul III in the Constitution *Licet*, July 21, 1542. The purpose for which this Supreme Congregation was established was to safeguard the purity and integrity of faith and morals.[4] Quite naturally, then, the Pauline Privilege soon came to be regarded as belonging to the scope of the Holy Office. When Pius X reformed the Roman Curia by the Constitution *Sapienti Consilio*, he made it clear that this Congregation alone had competence in cases of the Pauline Privilege,[5] and the law of the Code is most specific on this point.[6]

In the understanding and interpreting of the principle of canon 1127, the only safe guide to be followed is that which is set down by the decisions rendered by the Holy Office. Gasparri, in indicating the source of the legislation of canon 1127 in his edition of the Code, lists only such responses. And while these responses are not infallible doctrinal decisions, they are the norm to be followed in determining whether or not in such doubtful cases the favor of the law may be extended. To show that the principle in question has been consistently applied by the Holy Office it will be necessary to examine those responses in which that principle is either expressly stated or, at least, implied. No attempt will be made to follow a chronological order. Rather, the responses will be grouped according to the nature of the doubts they intend to solve. Those will be presented first

[3] Cf. Rayanna, "De Constitutione S. Pii Papae V, Romani Pontificis"—*Periodica*, XXVIII (1939), 25.

[4] Cappello, *De Curia Romana* (2 vols., Romae, 1911), I, 61.

[5] Cappello, *op. cit.*, I, 63.

[6] Canons 247; 1962.

which relate to doubts concerning the existence or the validity of a first marriage in infidelity; then those which relate to doubts about the fulfillment of the conditions established as essential for the certain application of the Pauline Privilege.

ARTICLE I. DOUBTFUL EXISTENCE OR DOUBTFUL VALIDITY OF INFIDEL MARRIAGES

To judge of the validity or invalidity of marriages contracted by infidels, particularly for places where polygamy is the custom, is a very difficult matter. Frequently it is impossible to reach a definite conclusion; the validity of the marriage remains in doubt. If the marriage in question is invalid, there is no difficulty; if the marriage is valid, the Pauline Privilege can be used; if the validity of the marriage remains in doubt, there is a grave problem affecting the necessity of making interpellations and the rights of the infidel which are uncertain.

The Holy See has never taken the view that there can be a presumption "in dubio standum est pro invaliditate matrimonii." The presumption has always been to the contrary. The formula used in marriage cases expresses the mind of the Church: "*An constat de nullitate matrimonii.*" In every case there must be an investigation to determine the status of the marriage.[7] Even among savage tribes this investigation must be made because, as the Holy Office pointed out, it is neither certain nor proved that there is no valid marriage among such tribes or that they have no idea of the distinction between marriage and concubinage. Such a judgment must come from particular facts ascertained by careful study. Therefore no general rule that such unions are invalid can be established. On the contrary, careful inquiry must be made in each particular case. Such is the burden of the instruction of the Holy Office to the Bishop of St.

[7] S.C.S. Off., instr. (ad Vic. Ap. Oceaniae Central.), 18 dec. 1872—*Fontes,* 1024; S.C.S. Off., instr. (ad Ep. S. Alberti), 9 dec. 1874, nn. 11, 16, 17;—*Fontes,* 1036; S.C.S. Off., instr. (ad Ep. Nesquallien.), 24 ian. 1877—*Fontes,* 1050; S.C.S. Off. (ad Vic Ap. Iaponiae Meridionalis), 4 febr. 1891—*Fontes,* n. 1130; S.C.S. Off., 18 maii 1892, ad 1—*Fontes,* n. 1156.

Albert.[8] Thus it must be determined whether or not there was any impediment of the natural, divine or civil law.[9] These instructions to the Bishops of St. Albert (later the see of Edmonton) and Nesqually (later the see of Seattle) insist upon an investigation as to the existence or non-existence of suspensive conditions contrary to the substance of a valid marriage.

Likewise, an investigation must be made concerning the fulfillment or non-fulfillment of the ceremonies customary in different countries, for the Holy Office has declared that "one must regard as valid those marriages which are celebrated with the usual ceremonies of the country, when the mutual and present consent of the parties has been sufficiently expressed according to the common estimation of the locality." [10] The Holy Office also warned that infidels sometimes marry without observing the customary ceremonies, but that in the course of time such a union may pass into a legitimate marriage.[11]

But despite careful examination it frequently happens that the doubt cannot be resolved. There is not sufficiently strong evidence to beget moral certainty either for the validity or for the invalidity of the marriage in question. In such circumstances if a doubt of fact is involved it is permitted in favor of the faith to accept the oath of an infidel that he has never entered a valid marriage, if after investigation his credibility is established, or if there is but slight doubt that he is trustworthy.[12] If there is serious doubt about the validity or the existence of a former marriage of an infidel, then in favor of the faith such a marriage may be regarded as invalid.[13]

[8] S.C.S. Off., 9 dec. 1874, ad 2-11—*Fontes,* n. 1036.

[9] S.C.S. Off., instr. (ad Ep. S. Alberti), 9 dec. 1874, ad 8-11—*Fontes,* n. 1036; S.C.S. Off., instr. (ad Ep. Nesquallien.), 24 ian. 1877—*Fontes,* n. 1050.

[10] S.C.S. Off. (Niger), 17 aug. 1898—*Fontes,* n. 1205.

[11] S.C.S. Off. (Siam), 22 nov. 1871—*Fontes,* n. 1019; S.C.S. Off., instr. (ad Ep. S. Alberti), 9 dec. 1874, ad 17—*Fontes,* n. 1036.

[12] S.C.S. Off. (Siouxormen.), 18 maii 1892, ad 1—*Fontes,* n. 1155.

[13] Ubi vero converti nolit, vel serio dubitetur de validitate matrimonii cum prima, poterunt quamlibet ducere, dummodo sit baptizata, renovato consensu. —SSmus. adprobavit. S.C.S. Off. Siouxormen.), 18 maii 1892, ad 2,—*Fontes,* n. 1155.

This doctrine of the Holy Office is not singular, for in 1836, in reply to a question sent by the Archbishop of Quebec requesting the extension of the Constitution *Romani Pontificis* of St. Pius V for use in Canada, the Holy Office declined the extension asked for and stated that, if the first marriage was valid, then the polygamist should return to his first wife. But when the validity of the first and of the subsequent marriages was doubtful, then the infidel upon his conversion could choose whichever of the women with whom he had lived, or any other woman, provided only that she too received baptism, and then contract marriage with her. Gregory XVI approved this decree, and to solve the problem in the case in which the first marriage had been valid, he granted the faculty to dispense from the required interpellations when they could not be made or when it was apparent that it would be of no use to make them.[14] The responses indicated below repeat in substance what has been already discussed; they insist on careful investigation and upon the fact that the doubts must be serious, and not mere negative doubts or vain fears.[15]

When, therefore, the existence or the validity of a marriage of infidels was insolubly doubtful, it was the confirmed practice of the Holy Office, with the approval of the Pope, to allow missionaries to regard such marriages as invalid when the favor of the faith was at stake.[16] If the marriage was considered as invalid, then neither the interpellations nor the dispensation from them seemed to be strictly necessary.[17] Yet it appeared to be a preferable policy to make the interpellations,[18] or to obtain a dispensation from them.[19]

[14] S.C.S. Off., 8 iun. 1836—*Fontes*, n. 874.

[15] S.C.S. Off., instr. (ad Vic. Ap. Oceaniae Centralis), 18 dec. 1872—*Fontes*, n. 1024; S.C.S. Off., instr. (ad Ep. S. Alberti), 9 dec. 1874—*Fontes*, n. 1036; S.C.S. Off. (Mongoliae), 29 nov. 1882—*Fontes*, n. 1075; S.C.S. Off. (ad Vic. Ap. Iaponiae Meridionalis), 4 febr. 1891—*Fontes*, n. 1130; S.C.S. Off. (Siouxormen.), 18 maii 1892—*Fontes*, n. 1155; S.C.S. Off. (Niger), 17 aug. 1898—*Fontes*, n. 1205.

[16] S.C.S. Off. (Zanguebar), 18 maii 1892, ad finem—*Fontes*, n. 1156.

[17] S.C.S. Off., instr. (ad Ep. S. Alberti), 9 dec. 1874—*Fontes*, n. 1036; S.C.S. Off. (Siouxormen.), 18 maii 1892—*Fontes*, n. 1155.

[18] S.C.S. Off., apr. 1899—*Fontes*, n. 1222.

[19] S.C.S. Off., 18 maii 1892—*Fontes*, n. 1156; S.C.S. Off., 16 aug. 1894—*Acta Sanctae Sedis* (ASS), XXIX (1894), 565. This was a case wherein

But in favor of the faith a marriage insolubly doubtful may also be regarded as valid. This, of course, could happen if both parties to such a union were bound by dubious bonds of former marriages and, since they were living peacefully together, wished upon conversion to renew their consent and so to validate their union. A doubtful marriage founded in infidelity could also be considered valid if only one party became baptized and wished to cohabit with the infidel. But in that case the cohabitation could be allowed only if there were no danger to the faith or morals of the convert because of the character of the infidel.[20]

Such cohabitation could be permitted even when it was impossible to obtain a definite matrimonial consent in view of the dangers that might arise if the infidel were asked to renew his consent. Baptism was not to be refused to an infidel, generally the woman, under such circumstances, since she was considered to be the true wife of the man in question. She was to be left in good faith until such time that the validity of the marriage could, with safety, be assured.[21]

It has already been noted that in the instruction to the Vicar Apostolic of Central Oceania express mention was made of Benedict XIV's rule that in doubtful matters the judgment should be in favor of the faith. And from this and the other cited instructions it is clear that this principle has been in constant use in the jurisprudence of the Holy Office as a safe and practical norm of action to settle difficulties which arose when it was impossible to determine the existence or the validity of a marriage contracted in infidelity. In favor of the faith such marriages could, according to the responses of the Holy Office, be considered as valid or as invalid according as the validity or the invalidity would open the way for conversion and baptism in the true Church.

a marriage was doubtful and the Holy Father granted a dispensation from the interpellations, "quatenus opus sit."

[20] S.C.S. Off., instr. (ad Vic. Ap. Oceaniae Central.), 18 dec. 1872—*Fontes*, n. 1024.

[21] S.C.S. Off., instr. (ad Vic. Ap. Oceaniae Central.), 18 dec. 1872—*Fontes*, n. 1024; S.C.S. Off., instr. (ad Ep. S. Alberti), 9 dec. 1874—*Fontes*, 1036.

Article II. Doubt and the Essential Conditions of the Pauline Privilege

There can be no question that the Holy Office employed the principle that the judgment in doubtful matters should be in favor of the faith in regard to the existence or the validity of infidel marriage. It is equally true that the Holy Office has applied that same principle to the dissolution of marriages, certainly and validly contracted, when the essential conditions for the application of the Pauline Privilege were only doubtfully fulfilled.

A. *Doubts Concerning the Departure of the Infidel*

One of the essential conditions, as has been shown, for the application of the Pauline Privilege is that the infidel has departed. This departure may be either physical or moral. Several responses of the Holy Office state that causes other than malice or hatred of the faith are sufficient, since the convert enjoys the favor of the faith. Should the infidel create an unhappy married life in which there constantly arise quarrels which are occasioned by the new religion of the convert, or if without being caused by the infidel party they have already been composed or condoned, then it is to be considered that a moral departure has taken place. If there remain any serious doubt regarding the absence of such conditions, then the doubt is to be settled in favor of the converted party.[22]

The same seems to be true according to a decision of the Holy Office if the convert after baptism has furnished a cause which warrants the infidel's departure, but the infidel, having already departed, knows nothing either of the faults of the convert or of the fact of the latter's conversion. For the Holy Office referred to its own decree of August 1, 1759, and to an instruction of the Congregation for the Propagation of the Faith which demanded the interpellations in a case wherein apparently the separation was quite possibly caused by the adultery of the convert. These instructions indicated that no inquiry was to be made as to whether the convert's expulsion preceeded

[22] S.C.S. Off. (Cochinchin), 1 aug. 1759—*Fontes*, n. 810; S.C.S. Off., 26 apr. 1899—*Fontes*, n. 1222.

or followed her act of adultery.[23] To these instructions it added the formula: *et ad mentem: Mens est ut in dubiis iudicium sit in fidei favorem.*[24]

B. *Doubts Concerning the Response to the Interpellations*

The necessity of the interpellations for the use of the Pauline Privilege has been briefly mentioned. Naturally it is to be presumed that the responses of the infidel have been given seriously and sincerely. But, if upon investigation, it is certain that the responses of the infidel party were given in bad faith, he may be treated as though he had refused conversion and peaceful cohabitation. In favor of the faith his affirmative answers may be treated as though they had been negative.[25]

In its decree of November 29, 1882, the Holy Office also indicated that if the infidel, upon being asked whether or not he wished to be converted, gave an indefinite reply, that is, one which referred to conversion in the vague future, the convert was not to be required to await the infidel's decision beyond six months, a rule approved by Sixtus V. For in favor of the faith this dubious reply was to be taken as negative because of the danger to the convert's faith.[26]

This reply also contains further forceful evidence of the application of the principle that in doubtful matters the decision is to be in favor of the faith. For in the fourth doubt presented for solution, it was asked: what was to be thought of a negative response to the interpellations which was obtained only indirectly, and not in reply to direct questions. The Holy Office, after consultation with the Holy Father (Leo XIII), stated that the marriages contracted on the strength of such responses were not to be disturbed, but that for the future the interpellations were to be made in the way prescribed by the Church. The value of the interpellations, made only indirectly,

[23] S. C. de Prop. Fide, instr., 16 ian. 1797—*Coll. S.C.P.F.*, n. 634; *Fontes*, n. 4652.

[24] S.C.S. Off., 19 apr. 1899—*Fontes*, n. 1220.

[25] S.C.S. Off. (Mongoliae), 29 nov. 1882, ad 2, 3—*Fontes*, n. 1075; S.C.S. Off., 16 aug. 1894—ASS, XXIX (1894), 564.

[26] *Fontes*, n. 1075; cf. also III Council (1582-1583), Synod of Lima, art. 2, c. 10—Mansi, XXXVI bis, 200.

was therefore dubious, and here evidently the Holy See followed the practice which it frequently used to handle doubtful cases, namely, that of dissolving the previous bond if it really existed.[27]

C. *Doubts Concerning Baptism*

Questions concerning the dissolution of marriages contracted between two doubtfully baptized non-Catholics, or between a doubtfully baptized non-Catholic and an infidel, or between a certainly baptized and a doubtfully baptized non-Catholic, present singular difficulties in relation to the application of the Pauline Privilege and the wider privilege of the faith.

Only those responses of the Holy Office which were given before the Code are in place here, as reflecting whether or not it was the mind of the Holy Office to solve doubts relative to baptism according to the principle that in doubt the judgment was to be favorable to the liberty of the convert. Other discussion on this point, as well as on many other possible doubts that may be settled in accordance with canon 1127, are treated in the canonical commentary; they are applications of this principle, not contributions to its history.

Careful search has discovered but one response on the solution of the problem caused by two doubtful baptisms. In 1872 the Vicar Apostolic of Central Oceania presented to the Holy Office the case of two doubtfully baptized heretics. One of them was converted and baptized in the Catholic Church. Shortly thereafter the unconverted spouse deserted the convert. In view of the very grave doubt concerning the validity of the former baptism, it was asked whether or not the convert might be considered as a convert from infidelity and, by means of the application of the Pauline Privilege, might be permitted to enter a new marriage. The Congregation answered in one unqualified word: "*Negative.*" Clearly it was the mind of the Congregation not to extend the favor of the faith to such a case.[28]

[27] S.C.S. Off. (Mongoliae), 29 nov. 1882, ad 4—*Fontes*, n. 1075; S.C.S. Off., 16 aug. 1894—ASS, XXIX, 564.

[28] "Utrum pars conversa propter gravissimum dubium de baptismo in heresi recepto aequiparari possit parti ab infidelitate conversae et propter Paulinum privilegium ad alias nuptias transire?" S.C. respondit: "Negative"

In regard to those cases in which only one of the parties was doubtfully baptized while the other was certainly unbaptized the pre-Code decisions have no present value. In the legislation before 1918 a doubtful baptism was presumed valid "*in ordine ad validitatem matrimonii.*" [29] As a result the Holy Office declared such marriages invalid because of the impediment of disparity of worship. The solution of such cases presents no great difficulty. If the baptism was in reality valid, then the marriage was invalid. If the doubtful baptism was in reality invalid, the marriage was only a legitimate marriage which was capable of dissolution in favor of the faith by the application of the supreme ministerial power of the Sovereign Pontiff which he exercised by approving the responses of the Holy Office. Such a solution is of no juridical interest to the larger question involved, namely, whether the Pauline Privilege could be so used. That is a problem intrinsically connected with the law of the Code; it will be treated fully in the Commentary.

The responses of the Holy Office here cited were intended to show that it has been the mind of the Holy Office, with the approval of the Holy Father, to solve doubts in regard to the complex problems of infidel marriages by applying the principle that in doubt the judgment is to be in favor of the faith. In the responses cited, the principle embodied in canon 1127 is certainly discernible. Often it is expressed; often it is implied. For it is in the jurisprudence of the Holy Office that the principle of canon 1127 finds its clearest and most direct source.

—S.C.S. Off., instr. (ad Vic. Ap. Oceaniae Centralis), 18 dec. 1872, ad 2—*Fontes*, n. 1024.

[29] Quaeritur: "Ad 1; Matrimonium dubie baptizati cum non baptizata estne validum?" Resp.: "Ad 1: Matrimonium esse habendum uti invalidum ob impedimentum disparitatis cultus."—S.C.S. Off. (Iaponiae), 14 iul. 1880, ad 1—*Fontes*, n. 1065. Cf. also S.C.S. Off., 7 iulii 1880, quoted in Wernz-Vidal, *Ius Matrimoniale*, V, n. 631, note 61; S.C.S. Off., 9 sept. 1868 (Iaponiae)—*Coll. S.C.P.F.*, n. 1334; *Fontes*, n. 1007; S.C.S. Off. (ad Vic. Ap. Iaponiae Merid.), 4 febr. 1891—*Coll. S.C.P.F.*, n. 1746—*Fontes*, n. 1130.

PART TWO

CANONICAL COMMENTARY

Chapter V

INTERPRETATION OF THE TERMS OF CANON 1127 "IN RE DUBIA PRIVILEGIUM FIDEI GAUDET FAVORE IURIS"

Since the promulgation of the Code of Canon Law, there has been but one general, authentic interpretation of the text of canon 1127, "in doubtful matters the privilege of the faith enjoys the favor of the law." This interpretation, which concerns the use of the Pauline Privilege by those who are doubtfully baptized, was given June 10, 1937,[1] by the Congregation of the Holy Office which alone is competent to decide matters which directly or indirectly, in law or in fact, are related to the Pauline Privilege and to the matrimonial impediments of disparity of worship and mixed religion.[2]

Except in relation to doubtful baptisms, therefore, the meaning of the canon must be determined according to the norms of canon 18. The legal phraseology in which the law has been cast should be understood in its proper sense with due regard to text and context. The doubts and obscurities which remain require that recourse be made, according to the secondary rules of interpretation, to a consideration of parallel passages in the Code, of the end and circumstances of the law, and inasmuch as it is the purpose of the interpretation of any law to discover the will of the lawgiver, of the mind of the legislator himself.[3]

It must be borne in mind also that a study of the historical background of canon 1127 clearly indicates that this legislation restates

[1] *Acta Apostolicae Sedis, Commentarium Officiale*, XXIX (1937), 305-306. Hereafter cited *AAS*.

[2] Canons 247, § 3; 1962.

[3] Canon 18. Cf. A. Van Hove, *Commentarium Lovaniense in Codicem Iuris Canonici*, Vol. I, tom. II, *De Legibus Ecclesiasticis* (Mechliniae-Romae: Dessain, 1930), n. 250.

the former law in its entirety. The interpretation of the canon is, then, governed necessarily by the provisions of canon 6, 2°.[4] Since the principle of canon 1127 is not new, it must be interpreted in accordance with former enactments, especially the decrees, instructions and the solutions of difficulties emanating from the Congregation of the Holy Office and from the Congregation for the Propagation of the Faith.[5]

Finally, canon 1127, like the Pauline Privilege and like the Constitution mentioned in canon 1125, is a law which in a very special way favors the Catholic faith in its inherent spiritual interests which compel men to accept it as the true religion of Christ. It is, therefore, to be interpreted widely, for such laws, even though they establish exceptions to the common law, are considered favorable, not odious, and are not to be given a strict interpretation.[6] Strict interpretation would understand the terms of the law in the least extended meaning of the proper sense as discovered by the use of the rules of interpretation. Wide interpretation, while retaining the proper sense, gives that sense the widest extension possible.[7] Canonists agree that the principle of canon 1127 should be given a wide rather than a strict interpretation.[8] From the very nature of the principle involved, the desirability of a broad interpretation is evident. It would be difficult to understand what benefit would accrue to the faith if this

[4] "Canones qui ius vetus ex integro referunt, ex veteris iuris auctoritate, atque ideo ex receptis apud probatos auctores interpretationibus, sunt aestimandi."

[5] Vromant, *Ius Missionariorum*, Vol. V, *De Matrimonio* (2. ed. Bruxellis et Parisiis: Museum Lessianum, 1938), n. 368; Cicognani, *Canon Law* (2. rev. ed., trans. by J. M. O'Hara and F. Brennan, Philadelphia: Dolphin Press, 1935), pp. 502-503.

[6] Cicognani, *Canon Law*, pp. 617-618; S.C. de Prop. Fide, resp. (C. P. pro Sin.—Cochinchin.) 2 iul., 1827 in fine—*Fontes*, n. 4738.

[7] Michiels, *Normae Generales Iuris Canonici* (2 vols. Lublin: Universitas Catholica, 1929), I, 380-381.

[8] Cappello, *De Matrimonio*, n. 788; Vermeersch-Creusen, *Epitome Iuris Canonici* (3 vols., Vol. I, 6. ed., Vols. II-III, 5. ed., Mechliniae, Romae: Dessain, 1934-1937), II, n. 437. This work will hereafter be cited as *Epitome*. Cf. also Vermeersch, "Interpretatio Canonis 1127,"—*Periodica*, X (1922), (25).

favor of the law were subjected to strict interpretation, or how such an interpretation could be reconciled with the terms and intent of the canon. In all of her decisions and instructions relative to the Pauline Privilege the Church has always maintained a benign attitude. In every possible way she wishes to make conversion and the practice of the true faith easy for the infidel.

With these general principles of interpretation in mind, one next finds it necessary to analyze the exact nature of the concepts as found in the law of canon 1127.

ARTICLE I. THE MEANING OF "PRIVILEGIUM FIDEI"

The term "privilege of the faith" has a multiple sense. It may be understood as a general principle conferring the right to choose in doubtful cases that probable solution which will be favorable to the acquisition or the preservation of the faith. It is in this sense that Benedict XIV applied the privilege of the faith in his letter *Probe te* of December 15, 1751.[9] But the principle of canon 1127 represents a specific application of this general principle, as its position in the Code indicates. The legislator has inserted it within the ambit of the article *De Dissolutione Vinculi*. This is the first article of Chapter X, *De Separatione Coniugum*, under the title on Matrimony in the third book of the Code. The *privilegium fidei* of canon 1127, therefore, directly affects only matrimonial problems. In this sense the term *privilegium fidei* is of ancient origin, for until comparatively recent times the term "privilege of the faith" was used exclusively to indicate the Pauline Privilege.[10]

In its strict sense, the "privilege of the faith" is understood as the faculty granted to a convert from infidelity through power divinely bestowed, whereby the convert may contract a second marriage after the reception of baptism, if his infidel consort departs, that is, if the

[9] *Fontes*, n. 418. Cf. Cappello, *De Matrimonio*, n. 788, nota 75; Creusen, "Baptême Douteux et Mariage Indissoluble,"—*NRT*, LII (1925), 229; Léry, *Le Privilège de la Foi*, n. 1. Cf. also *supra*, Chapter II.

[10] Jelicic, "De Privilegio Fidei eiusque Fundamento Iuridico"—*Jus Pontificium*, XVII (1937), 145; Vermeersch, "Quaesita de usu privilegii fidei,"—*Periodica*, XVII (1928) 241*-243*.

latter refuses to be baptized or at least to live peacefully with the convert without blaspheming God. Indeed, some authors apply canon 1127 only to the doubts about the fulfillment of the necessary conditions for the use of the Pauline Privilege or the privilege of the faith in its strict sense, for these terms are identical.[11]

But such a restriction seems to be unwarranted, for in canon 1120 the Code mentions the term "Pauline Privilege" expressly. In canons 1069 and 1127, however, the term "privilege of the faith" is employed. And while the application of canon 1127 is far more frequent in relation to the Pauline Privilege, it does not follow that the legislator intended to restrict its use to the Pauline Privilege. For in its wide sense, the privilege of the faith extends not only to the Pauline Privilege but also to the plenitude of the vicarious or ministerial power in virtue of which the Roman Pontiff may, and in fact does, dissolve the bond of marriage when such a bond would be an obstacle to conversion or to the practice of the faith, on condition that the welfare of souls demands the use of this power, that such dissolutions are not the occasion of scandal and that it is evident that the marriage was not consummated after the baptism of both parties.

Canon 1127, then, would apply not only to the Pauline Privilege but also to the provisions of canon 1125 and to those dissolutions of the natural bond of marriage between a person baptized in heresy and one who is certainly baptized. For to the privilege of the faith in the wide sense must be referred: 1) the apostolic power of the Supreme Pontiff to dissolve a legitimate marriage entered into and consummated in infidelity, when conditions required for the use of the Pauline Privilege are only doubtfully fulfilled, or where they certainly are not fulfilled; 2) the power used by the Holy Father time and again to dissolve, in favor of the faith, a marriage validly entered into and consummated by a party baptized in heresy with an unbaptized person, if one of the parties is converted to the Catholic

[11] De Smet, *De Sponsalibus et Matrimonio*, n. 255; Vromant, "Le Privilège de la Foi au Canon 1127,"—*NRT*, LIX (1932), 441; Vermeersch-Creusen, *Epitome*, II, n. 437; "Commentaire au Canon 1127,"—L'Ami du Clergé, XLII (1925), 221.

faith;[12] 3) the power which Gregory XIII used in the Constitution, *Populis*,[13] to dissolve, in favor of the faith, marriages contracted and consummated in infidelity which, upon the conversion and the baptism of both parties, had become sacramental, but which had not again been consummated after they had taken on the sacramental character. Therefore, the Pauline Privilege is, as it were, a species under the generic privilege of the faith, which has no limitations except the limitations of the supreme power of the Pope, and which extends to every marriage which is not consummated, sacramental marriage.[14] There is no valid reason to restrict the term *privilegium fidei* in canon 1127. Rather, both the rules of interpretation and the authority of canonists extend the application of the canon to the widest meaning of the term.[15]

Article II. The Notion of favor iuris

A. *Canon 1014*

The meaning of the term "favor of the law" employed in canon 1127 must be considered in its relation to the same term found in canon 1014.[16] As is readily evident, canon 1014 is the pivotal point of all matrimonial procedure. No matter on what score a marriage

[12] It was the change in the impediment of disparity of worship according to canon 1070, § 1, which gave rise to such cases.

[13] Docum. VIII, *C.I.C.*

[14] Canon 1118: "Matrimonium validum ratum et consummatum nulla humana potestate nullaque causa, praeterquam morte, dissolvi potest."

[15] Cappello: "Hoc principium (canon 1127) respicit tum Privilegium Paulinum tum usum potestatis vicariae Romani Pontificis quatenus refertur ad omnes casus quibus certo applicari nequit illud privilegium et qui subsunt potestati vicariae Papae," *De Matrimonio*, n. 788; Arendt, "Quomodo in favorem fidei solvatur a S. Pontifice matrimonium in infidelitate contractum, nota theologica-canonica circa canonem 1127,"—*Ephemerides Theologicae Lovanienses* (hereafter *ETL*), I (1924), p. 184; Wernz-Vidal, *Ius Matrimoniale*, n. 637 in fine; Payen, *De Matrimonio in Missionibus*, nn. 2205-2206 bis.

[16] Canon 1014: "Matrimonium gaudet favore iuris: quare in dubio standum est pro valore matrimonii, donec contrarium probetur, salvo praescripto can. 1127."

is attacked, the plaintiff is immediately confronted with the law there established. There are two consequences of this principle: 1. when a marriage has evidently been contracted, it must be considered valid until its nullity has been fully proven; 2. when the fact that a marriage has been contracted is not evident, if the so-called marriage has the semblance of true marriage, it must be so regarded until the contrary is fully proved.[17]

The plaintiff, therefore, is forced to prove either that the so-called matrimonial contract which is being contested has not the semblance of marriage and never was entered into, or that the marriage was invalid from the beginning.[18] The principle enunciated in canon 1014 applies to all marriages. Because of the sacramental nature of Christian marriage, it applies with special force; but the principle is also applicable to marriage contracted even by the unbaptized.[19] Whether the doubt arises in relation to the fact or the existence of a marriage, or in relation to its validity, canon 1014 is to be applied. For the law governs human affairs where there is always the possibility of error and fraud. The canon, therefore, favors the marriage by taking it into possession and guarding it strongly.

Consequently, canon 1014 is both in wording and operation, a typical presumption of law.[20] But it must be noted that this principle is not merely a presumption of ecclesiastical legislation. It is, rather, an unvarying norm based on divine law. The indissolubility of the marriage contract, whether sacramental or legitimate, does not depend on the will of the Church. The Church, therefore, could

[17] Cappello, *De Matrimonio*, n. 51.

[18] Chelodi, *Ius Matrimoniale* (4. ed., recognita et aucta a Vigilio Dalpiaz, Tridenti: A. Ardesi, 1937), n. 7.

[19] S.C.S. Off., instr. (ad Vic. Ap. Oceaniae Cent.), 18 dec. 1872—*Fontes*, n. 1024; Cappello, *De Matrimonio*, n. 53; Gasparri, *Tractatus Canonicus de Matrimonio* (editio nova ad mentem codicis I. C., 2 vols., Typis Polyglottis Vaticanis, 1932), n. 18. Hereafter *De Matrimonio*.

[20] Manning, *Presumptions of Law in Marriage Cases*, The Catholic University of America Canon Law Studies, n. 94, (Washington, D. C.: The Catholic University of America, 1935), p. 53.

not recede from the principle of canon 1014, nor sanction its contrary, without grave danger of violating divine law.[21]

B. *Canon 1127*

The general principle of canon 1014, that in doubt, the validity of marriage is to be upheld until nullity is fully proved, is subject to one exception expressed in the canon itself. For the legislator safeguarded the principle of canon 1127, "in doubtful matters the privilege of the faith enjoys the favor of the law." Canon 1014 does not comprehend those cases wherein there is question of conversion to the Catholic faith and the reception of baptism.[22] In canon 1127, then, the term "favor of the law," objectively considered, is to be understood as the disposition of the law to admit the use of the privilege of the faith in a doubtful matter concerning marriage. The presumption in favor of the validity of a marriage, which is to be upheld in face of a doubt of law or of fact concerning its validity, yields to a presumption in favor of the faith, or to the liberty of a convert free from infidelity.[23] When both parties of a marriage contracted in infidelity become by baptism subject to the Sovereign Pontiff, or even if one alone becomes subject, and the Pauline Privilege cannot *certainly* be applied, then in virtue of canon 1127 the legitimate marriage so contracted may in a case of doubt be considered valid or invalid in accordance with what the favor of the faith suggests as a solution for the spiritual benefit of the convert.[24]

21 Cappello, "Quaestiones Peculiares de Re Matrimoniali," *Jus Pontificium*, XX (1940), pp. 27-28.

22 Cappello, *De Matrimonio*, n. 55; *idem*, "Quaestiones Peculiares de Re Matrimoniali,"—*Jus Pontificium*, XX (1940), pp. 29-30; Wernz-Vidal, *Ius Matrimoniale*, n. 44; Vermeersch-Creusen, *Epitome*, II, n. 437; Cerato, *Matrimonium a Codice I. C. Integre Desumptum* (4. ed., Patavii: Typis Seminarii Patavini, 1929), n. 3. Hereafter cited *Matrimonium*.

23 S.C.S. Off., instr. (ad Ep. S. Alberti), 9 dec. 1874—*Fontes*, n. 1036; S.C.S. Off., instr. (ad Vic. Ap. Oceaniae Cent.), 18 dec. 1872—*Fontes*, n. 1024.

24 Vromant, *Commentarium in Facultates Apostolicas*, n. 83; Vermeersch, "Interpretatio Canonis 1127,"—*Periodica*, X (1922), p. (26); Wernz-Vidal, *Ius Matrimoniale*, n. 631.

Canon 1127, therefore, may also be understood as a presumption of law in relation to all marriages which are capable of dissolution within the limits of the privilege of the faith. Triebs' statement that canon 1127 constitutes a *presumptio iuris et de iure,*[25] does not seem to be correct.[26] His opinion is based on the dissolution of the bond contracted in infidelity. This bond cannot be reinstated, so he observes, once it has been dissolved to pave the way for the second marriage, for the contraction of the second marriage becomes definitively permanent. Obviously that is true. If the conditions for the valid use of the Pauline Privilege are doubtful and the privilege of the faith is applied, then a marriage which under canon 1014 would have to be presumed valid becomes dissolved. However, should it be discovered later that one or both parties in whose favor canon 1127 was evoked had successfully concealed facts and by fraud had obtained an apparent dissolution of the bond when in reality, the privilege of the faith was inapplicable, even though both parties had married again, the bond of the former marriage would necessarily have to be upheld. Triebs' view would imply that once canon 1127 has been applied to solve a marriage case, then the solution given would become an adjudicated matter. This is never true of marriage cases, except with regard to the civil effects.[27]

However, it is evident that canon 1127 is not merely a presumption of positive ecclesiastical law. Its nature and the effects of its application prove clearly that it is based on and governed by divine law.[28] Vermeersch points out that the legislator has made no distinction which would limit the favor of the law of canon 1127 to purely ecclesiastical law and hence such a distinction is not to be made.[29] But a far more conclusive argument can be advanced. The sentence of an ecclesiastical tribunal that the invalidity of a marriage

[25] Cf. canon 1826.

[26] *Praktisches Handbuch des geltenden kanonischen Eherechts in Vergleichung mit dem deutschen staatlichen Eherecht* (Breslau: Ostdeutsche Verlagsanstalt, 1933) p. 725.

[27] Canons 1903, 1989.

[28] Cappello, *De Matrimonio*, n. 788; idem, "Quaestiones Peculiares de Re Matrimonali," *Jus Pontificium*, XX (1940), 29.

[29] "Interpretatio Canonis 1127,"—*Periodica*, X (1922), (25)-(26).

is not evident from the proofs adduced, certainly does not change the objective reality. Necessarily the marriage is either valid or invalid. To maintain that canon 1127 means that in cases of doubt the ecclesiastical judge may safely declare a marriage invalid would be to maintain that in favor of the faith the judge by his sentence could change the objective order of truth. The juridical explanation of the exception to canon 1014 as granted by canon 1127 is quite different. A valid marriage contracted in infidelity can be dissolved only by the use of the Pauline Privilege or by the wider privilege of the faith. But, admittedly, the essential conditions of the Pauline Privilege are only doubtfully fulfilled. The solution of the doubt, therefore, can be attributed only to the ministerial power of the Pope, which he received directly from Almighty God and which he exercises in His name. This means that the favor of the divine law expressed as positive ecclesiastical law is necessary to explain the law in canon 1127.[30]

Article III. The Notion of *res dubia*

A. *Definition of Doubt in Relation to Canon 1127*

Doubt may be viewed in the strict sense of the philosopher or in its broader canonical acceptation. Philosophically, doubt is a state of mind in which the mind hesitates between two contradictory propositions and feels incapable of giving forthright assent to either of them. Of itself doubt signifies a purely internal psychological attitude; the mind alone judges about facts. The action of the mind has no influence on the facts themselves. Thus a proposition which is regarded as doubtful is one in regard to which sufficient evidence is not available. In itself the proposition is true or false. If the doubt resides in a mind equipped with due knowledge, it is called objective; if in a mind lacking due knowledge, the doubt is called subjective.[31]

[30] Wernz-Vidal, *Ius Matrimoniale*, n. 44; De Smet, *De Sponsalibus et Matrimonio*, n. 355; Arendt, "Nota circa canonem 1127,"—*ETL*, I (1924), 180-181: Creusen, "Baptême Douteux et Mariage Indissoluble,"—*NRT*, LII (1925), 235-236; Vromant, *De Matrimonio*, n. 368.

[31] Blat, *Commentarium Textus Codicis Iuris Canonici* (6 vols. Romae: Ferrari, 1921-1927), I, n. 72.

The term *res dubia,* as employed in canon 1127, contrasts sharply with the wording of canon 209, "*aut in dubio positivo et probabili.*"[32] This is an indication that a broad interpretation is conceded in canon 1127. However, canon 1127 may not be invoked unless the doubt in question is positive. A positive doubt must be to some extent objective; if the doubt were purely subjective or negative, there would be no question of the presence of anything but ignorance.[33] Certainly, ignorance could not be the basis of the application of the principle in question.[34] To apply canon 1127, then, there must be present a reason with some degree of probability in it for following either opinion. The doubt need not be one which demands grave as well as probable reasons on both sides of the question. It is sufficient that the doubt which persists after serious investigation according to the circumstances of time and place should exclude moral certainty concerning the truth of one side or the other.[35] From the nature of the principle of canon 1127 the doubt must be, morally considered, insoluble; if it is at all possible to arrive at certainty, this must be done. The Holy Office insists on a careful investigation which cannot be omitted in a matter of such great importance.[36]

A doubt may be either a doubt of fact or a doubt of law. A doubt of law exists when there is no certainty about the existence, permanence, force or comprehension of the law.[37] A doubt of fact exists when the existence and theoretical comprehension of the law are certain, but the existence of the fact or circumstances juridically

[32] Vermeersch-Creusen, *Epitome,* II, n. 437.

[33] Michiels, *Normae Generales,* I, 332, note 3.

[34] Cappello, *De Matrimonio,* n. 788; Payen, *De Matrimonio in Missionibus,* n. 2415 bis.

[35] Arendt, "Nota circa canonem 1127,"—*ETL,* I (1924), p. 181, n. 25; Vromant, *Ius Matrimoniale* (1. ed. 1931), n. 368; Payen, *De Matrimonio in Missionibus,* n. 2415 *bis.*

[36] S.C.S. Off., 18 maii 1892, ad 1, 2: "Instituendum est in singulis casibus particularibus examen circumstantiarum et modi quo coniugium primitus initum fuerit. Si vero pars una convertatur post conversionem alterius, et examinato casu particulari supersit dubium, stet pro nullitate matrimonii in favorem fidei."—*Fontes,* n. 1156.

[37] Toso, *Ad Codicem Iuris Canonici Commentaria Minora* (5 vols., Vol. I.) (2. ed., Romae, 1921), I, 42.

required for the assumption of its existence in a given case are not certain.[38] De Smet proposes an example of a doubt of law in relation to canon 1127. The case is concerned with a marriage contracted in infidelity between a brother and his sister. The marriage is probably invalid in the light of the natural law. If one of the parties upon conversion wished to marry again, the former marriage could be declared invalid; the use of the Pauline Privilege would not be necessary. If the doubt relates to the verification of one of the conditions necessary for the application of the Pauline Privilege, then the doubt is one of fact. In either doubt the principle of canon 1127 is applicable. But this canon may be employed only after serious and diligent investigation; if it be possible the doubt must be dissipated.

B. *Specification of the* RES DUBIA

In general it may be stated that canon 1127 may be applied whenever doubt arises in any way, whether the doubt relate to law or to fact, and regardless of whether the fact concern persons or circumstances. Chelodi, for example, in the third edition (1921) of his work *Ius Matrimoniale* [39] stated simply: "At certum est Privilegium Paulinum etiam in re dubia partem conversam iuvare quia gaudet favore iuris, iuxta perpetuam regulam canonicae iurisprudentiae." Vlaming also was very brief in his statement of the principle in question.[40]

Other authors, however, append to their commentaries on canon 1127 a catalogue of specific matters which after careful examination may remain insolubly doubtful. Since these are the matters which represent the ambit of the practical application of the principle of canon 1127 and which, therefore, must be considered thoroughly in the course of this study, it is intended here, for the sake of complete-

[38] Michiels, *Normae Generales*, I, 333.

[39] Cf. n. 156.

[40] *Praelectiones*, n. 733: " . . . dubium quod aut de valore prioris vinculi, aut de verificatis conditionibus privilegii Paulini applicandi, aut denique de verificatis adiunctis canonis 1125, remaneat, id solvendum est in favorem partis ad fidem conversae."

ness, merely to enumerate them without attempting to comment upon them in detail. It may be noted that the enumerations found in all the commentaries are practically in accord with one another. The following list, therefore, with a few unimportant modifications sometimes made, may be considered typical.

The doubts may concern:

1. the existence of a marriage reputed to have been contracted in infidelity;
2. the validity of a marriage certainly contracted in infidelity;
3. the dissolution of a marriage contracted in infidelity;
4. the fulfillment of the conditions necessary for the valid use of the Pauline Privilege by a former infidel who has been baptized in the Catholic faith:
   a. the sufficiency of the cause for dispensing from the interpellations or for awaiting the unbaptized party's reply;
   b. the interpretation of the meaning of an ambiguous reply to the interpellations;
   c. the sincerity of the infidel party's reply;
   d. the question whether or not the departure of the infidel was occasioned by a just cause;
5. the identity of the first wife of a polygamist; or of the first husband of a polyandrous woman;
6. the doubtful baptism received by one party.

To present individually each author's enumeration of these specific matters, which even after diligent examination may remain doubtful, would involve much repetition and would serve no useful purpose. The citations indicated below will enable the reader to make any comparisons which may perhaps be deemed necessary.[41]

[41] Vermeersch-Creusen, *Epitome*, II, n. 437; Wernz-Vidal, *Ius Matrimoniale*, n. 631; Vromant, *Ius Matrimoniale* (2. ed., 1938), nn. 368-381; idem, *Commentarium in Facultates Apostolicas*, nn. 84-85; Vermeersch, "Interpretatio Canonem 1127,"—*Periodica*, X (1922), p. (27); Arendt, "Nota circa canonem 1127,"—*ETL*, I (1924), 182-184; Cappello, *De Matrimonio*, n. 788; Cerato, *Matrimonium*, n. 127; Farrugia, *De Matrimonio et Causis Matrimonialibus* (Romae, 1924), n. 326; Gasparri, *De Matrimonio* (ed. 1932), n. 1168: Chelodi, *Ius Matrimoniale* (4. ed.), n. 156, nota 2; Triebs, *Kan. Eherecht*, p. 724; Schönsteiner, *Grundriss des kirchlichen Eherechts* (2. ed. revised, Wien: Ludwig Auer, 1937), pp. 838-840.

CHAPTER VI

THE JURIDIC BASIS OF CANON 1127

From the words in which it is expressed canon 1127 presupposes a doubt, whether of law or of fact, in relation to a marriage contracted in infidelity. If this doubt is found after careful examination to be insoluble, then by virtue of canon 1127 such a marriage may be considered valid or invalid according as the favor of the faith may be at stake.[1] But it is impossible to maintain that the principle of canon 1127 is based on arbitrary acceptance of validity or invalidity. Subjective doubt cannot change objective facts. To hold that it could would imply that a marriage objectively valid could become invalid merely by the decision that the favor of the faith called for a judgment of nullity.[2] Indeed, Wernz, in commenting on several decisions of the Holy Office to which were added the words, "mens est, ut in dubio iudicium sit in favorem fidei,"[3] pointed out that, while the meaning of these responses was clear, the reasons on which they were based were not equally clear.[4] Contemporary canonists refer the intrinsic reason and the dogmatic foundation of canon 1127 to the supreme, ministerial power of the Pope over all marriages that are not consummated sacramental marriages, when at least one of the parties becomes by baptism a subject of the Church, and the good of the faith demands the intervention of the Holy Father.[5] It will, therefore, be necessary to treat briefly of the exist-

[1] Vromant, *Commentarium in Facultates Apostolicas*, n. 83; Vermeersch, "Interpretatio Canonis 1127"—Periodica, X (1922), p. (26); Wernz-Vidal, Ius Matrimoniale, n. 631.

[2] Dalpiaz, "Annotationes in Decretum Sancti Officii die 10 iunii 1937,"—*Apollinaris*, X (1937, 337; Vromant, "Le Privilège de la Foi au Canon 1127,"—*NRT*, LIX (1932), 440; Wernz-Vidal, *Ius Matrimoniale*, n. 44, also n. 631, p. 757, note 61.

[3] S.C.S. Off., 18 maii 1892, ad 1, 2,—*Fontes*, n. 1155; S.C.S. Off., 26 apr. 1899—*Fontes*, n. 1222.

[4] Wernz, *Ius Matrimoniale*, n. 696.

[5] De Smet, *De Sponsalibus et Matrimonio* (4. ed.) n. 355; Wernz-Vidal, *Ius Matrimoniale*, nn. 44, 631; Payen, *De Matrimonio in Missionibus* (2. ed.), n. 2415—bis, p. 758; Arendt, "Nota circa canonem 1127,"—*ETL*, I

ence and the extent of this power of the Church over the marriage bond.

Article I. The Development of the Doctrine of Papal Dispensation

Until after the Reformation the question of the dissolution of marriages contracted in infidelity was confined to the application of the Pauline Privilege. Such marriages were recognized as lacking the supreme degree of stability which the Sacrament of Matrimony gives to Christian marriage; but theologians agreed that the bond could be broken in no other way than by the remarriage of the convert after the refusal of the infidel to be converted or, at least, to cohabit without blasphemy of Almighty God.[6] For natural law, together with the positive law of God as expressed in both the Old and the New Testament,[7] determines that even the legitimate marriage of infidels is intrinsically indissoluble.[8] The primary end of marriage, namely the begetting of children together with their education demands this stability.

But with the opening of the vast new mission fields consequent upon the discoveries of the Spanish and Portugese explorers at the end of the fifteenth century, new and unfamiliar problems urged a reconsideration of this point. In this way the doctrine of marriage relative to unions contracted in infidelity received new and unexpected development. The essence of this development is contained in the constitutions of Paul III, (*Altitudo*, June 1, 1537), of St. Pius V (*Romani Pontificis*, August 2, 1571) and of Gregory XIII (*Populis*, January 25, 1585). The former limited application of these constitutions is now extended to the whole Church by canon 1125

(1924), 180-181; Creusen, "Baptême Douteux et Mariage Indisoluble,"—*NRT*, LII (1925), 235-236.

[6] Joyce, *Christian Marriage*, p. 490.

[7] Gen., II: 23, 24; Matt., V: 31, 32; Matt., XIX: 3-9; Mark, X: 9; Luke, XVI: 18; I Cor., VII: 10, 11. Cf. O'Connor, "The Indissolubility of a Ratified Consummated Marriage,"—*ETL* (1936), 696-701.

[8] Sanchez, *De Matrimonio*, lib. II, disp. XIII, n. 7.

of the Code of Canon Law.[9] They are partially quoted in the Code as documents VI, VII, VIII.

Since these constitutions must be considered under other aspects later, it is intended only to point out that they granted dissolution of marriages contracted in infidelity without exacting the conditions demanded by St. Paul.[10] For Paul III, in addressing his Constitution *Altitudo* to the bishops of West and South India, granted to converts who before their conversion had had several wives the privilege of accepting the one whom they wished to receive, provided that such converts could not remember which wife they had taken first.[11] No consideration was shown for the infidel; there was no mention, naturally, that interpellations needed to be made. If the convert could not remember which was his first wife, he was free after his baptism to enter a new marriage.

The Constitution *Romani Pontificis* of St. Pius V treated of the situation of certain Indian people among whom polygamy and frequent divorce were widespread. The Pope stated that it would often be extremely difficult to find the first wife, and permitted the convert to retain the wife who received baptism with him. It has always been the teaching of the Church that the first marriage alone is valid. Hence, by implication the Pope pronounced the dissolution of a valid marriage, founded in infidelity, without exacting the conditions demanded by St. Paul.[12]

The Constitution *Populis* of Gregory XIII went even further. It was issued to meet difficulties caused by the African slave trade. Thousands of men were taken from their homes with no regard for family ties, and shipped to Spanish and Portugese possessions in America. The work of the missionaries among them was hampered seriously because of the fact that many of the prospective converts had previously been married. Though it was most desirable that

[9] Canon 1125: "Ea quae Matrimonium respiciunt in constitutionibus Pauli III . . . ; S. Pii V . . . ; Gregory XIII . . . , quaeque pro peculiaribus locis scripta sunt, ad alias quoque regiones in eisdem adiunctis extenduntur."

[10] I Cor., VII: 12-15.

[11] Burton, *A Commentary on Canon 1125*, pp. 38-39.

[12] Joyce, *Christian Marriage*, p. 490; Burton, *A Commentary on Canon 1125*, pp. 153-156.

they should have Christian wives, yet the former marriages caused grave difficulties. Often the convert did not know what had become of his wife. She had possibly been captured and taken across the sea; she could also possibly have become a member of the Church in the meantime.

Gregory XIII took account of all these difficulties. The Pope believed that the unions contracted during infidelity were true marriages, but not so firm that, if necessity demanded it, they could not be dissolved. Hence he granted to the local ordinaries of the specified districts, and to the missionaries and the members of the Society of Jesus who labored there, provided that the latter were approved by their superiors to hear confessions, faculties by which they could dispense from interpellations under these circumstances. This dispensation enabled the convert who was married before his baptism to contract marriage with a Catholic after baptism, provided that at least summary extrajudicial evidence was produced to show that the first wife could not be interpellated, or that, if she was interpellated, she did not give answer in the specified time. Gregory added:

> "Moreover, these marriages are never to be recinded even though it become known afterwards that the infidel was prevented by a just cause from declaring his or her intention, and had even become a convert at the time of the second marriage, but in virtue of our decree shall remain valid and firm and the offspring shall be legitimate." [13]

Here again the dissolution of a marriage founded in infidelity was by implication granted without the exacting of the conditions of the Pauline Privilege.

Since the Pauline Privilege was the one explicit means granted by the New Testament by which the bond of a marriage contracted and consummated by infidels could be dissolved, it was inevitable that theologians and canonists should make comparisons between the constitutions of Paul III, St. Pius V and Gregory XIII on the one hand, and the privilege of St. Paul on the other. It is not surprising that they should attempt to fit these privileges to the terms of the Pauline

[13] Document VIII of the Code. English translation from Burton, A *Commentary on Canon 1125*, p. 165.

Privilege. For, at the opening of the seventeenth century, the opinion that the Pope had the power to dissolve an infidel marriage in favor of the faith was far from the common teaching of the canonists. Basilius Pontius, O.S.A. (1570-1629), an eminent theologian and canonist, was bitterly opposed to this opinion. He taught that the indissolubility of marriage was derived entirely from the natural law and that the symbolism attaching to Christian marriage furnished no added firmness to the indissoluble character ofmarriage.[14] As far as any papal power was concerned, so he contended, a consummated, infidel marriage was as indissoluble as a consummated Christian marriage.[15]

Pontius' eminence did much to influence later thought on this subject. Cardinal Lambertini, later Benedict XIV, agreed with Pontius' view. He understood the grants of Paul III, St. Pius V and Gregory XIII, as "tempering the rigorous practice of interpellations" by allowing dispensations from the interpellations.[16] Benedict XIV used this phrase in reference to the Constitution of Gregory XIII; but his opinion was the same in regard to the Constitution of St. Pius V.[17]

A comparison of the enactments of these constitutions with the fundamental requirements of the Pauline Privilege shows that on the point of identical import the differences between them are irreconcilible. St. Pius V, indeed, did not even make any mention of interpellations or of dispensations from them. Yet it could have happened that the first wife might have been found and that she would have been willing to cohabit peacefully with her convert husband and this would have eliminated the application of the Pauline Privilege.

[14] Pontius, *De Sacramento Matrimonii Tractatus*, lib. I, cap. XIII.

[15] *Op. cit.*, lib. IX, cap. II, nn. 8, 11, 12: "Ego semper existimavi omnino certum matrimonium infidelium consummatum non posse dissolvi auctoritate Pontificis. Et quidem hanc fuisse hactenus communem Doctorum sententiam . . . dubitari non potest."

[16] *Quaestiones Canonicae*, q. 546, n. 38—*Opera Omnia* (17 vols. in 18, Prati, 1839-1847), XIII, 253.

[17] *De Synodo Dioecesana* (2 vols., Romae, 1767), lib. XIII, cap. XXI, nn. 4-6.

Gregory XIII, in the Constitution *Populis* demanded that the requirements of the Pauline Privilege be fulfilled wherever this was possible. Yet he also granted the faculty to dispense from the interpellations when they could not be made. The true intent of his Constitution becomes even clearer when it is realized that the validity of the new marriage was to be upheld even if at the time of her husband's second marriage the first wife had received the Sacrament of Baptism. St. Paul's provision was made for infidels; to include one of the faithful under the term "infidel" would have implied then, as now, an extension of the Pauline Privilege beyond its limits as laid down by St. Paul. And if the Pauline Privilege is, as some authors insisted,[18] the sole exception made by God to a law which under all other circumstances is of the strictest obligation, then its limits had to be accepted then, as now in the manner in which they were laid down. Not even the Pope could have extended or restricted the divine law by his interpretation.

But if the Pauline Privilege was both instituted and promulgated by St. Paul in view of the power he shared as an Apostle, then its extension requires only a participation in the same apostolic authority; such an extension is, then, in reality, a new law applying to cases not included under the former privilege. And this surely seems to be the natural and obvious sense of the constitutions; otherwise it would be difficult to understand why the Constitution *Romani Pontificis* should contain such fortifying clauses as "*motu proprio et ex certa scientia nostra, ac Apostolicae potestatis plenitudine,*" or why the Constitution *Populis* should contain clauses of similar sense.[19] Moreover, there is no question about the power of the Pope to dissolve the unconsummated marriages of Christians. Yet Christ raised to the dignity of a sacrament the contract which arises from the exchange of matrimonial consent between two baptized persons.[20] Sacramental marriage is a title to grace; it is a symbol of Christ's union with His Church. But as long as the marriage remains unconsum-

[18] Wernz, *Ius Matrimoniale*, n. 705; Wernz-Vidal, *Ius Matrimoniale*, n. 635.

[19] Gury-Ballerini, *Compendium Theologiae Moralis* (2. ed., Romae-Taurini, 1869), II, 522, 535; Cappello, *De Matrimonio*, n. 787.

[20] Canon 1012, § 1.

mated, its sacramental symbolism remains incomplete. Alexander III (1159-1181), in two decretals, taught that the entrance into religion of one party to a non-consummated Christian marriage dissolved the bond of marriage in such a way that the other party was free to marry again.[21] From the time of Martin V (1417-1431) the Holy See also granted dispensations in ratified unconsummated marriages.[22] *A fortiori*, then, the Pope can dissolve also the consummated marriages of infidels. Only in a most restricted sense can such marriages be said to represent the supernatural union of Christ with His Church. They convey no gift of grace; nor is their purpose the multiplication of the children of God. St. Thomas Aquinas notes the relative weakness of infidel marriages.[23] Gregory XIII indicated this weakness as the reason which justified his bestowal of the faculty of dispensing. If the Pope can dissolve an unconsummated sacramental marriage, much more can he dissolve a marriage in which one of the parties remains in unbelief. This, of course, is a power which the Pope would not use indiscriminately. The indissolubility of marriage is a divine law; the Holy Father dissolves a union only when he has a just cause to judge that God would want him to grant an exception. There are cases in which conversion to the true faith, and consequently the way of eternal salvation, would be too difficult if dissolution were not possible. In such instances the Pope intervenes *in favorem fidei* to sever a bond which lacks the indissolubility of a consummated marriage between the baptized.

Article II. The Basis of the Papal Power

It is quite evident that the provision of canon 1127 demonstrates the need of the Papal power to dissolve legitimate marriage.[24] The proof that the Pope has this power rests upon the use which has been

[21] Cc. 2, 7, X, *de conversione coniugatorum*, III, 32.

[22] Perrone, *De Matrimonio Christiano*, lib. III, c. VI, art. IV, I; Cajetan, *Opuscula Omnia D. Thomae de Vio in Tres Distincta Tomos* Lugduni, 1585), tractatus XXVIII, *De Matrimonio*, pp. 122-124.

[23] *Divi Thomae Aquinatis Opera* (2. ed., 28 vols., Venetiis, 1775- 1788), *IV Sent.*, dist. XXXIX, q. un., art. 5, ad 1.

[24] Payen, *De Matrimonio in Missionibus*, n. 2448.

made of it,[25] not only in the constitutions just considered, but in cases similar to that known as the "Helena Case." [26] Certainly, no one could maintain successfully that there is any question here of the application of a reflex principle to settle the doubt in question. There is present here the absolute necessity of safeguarding the validity of an action to be placed; there may be present the danger of violating the strict right of a third person. Either of these factors would exclude the use of probabalism.[27]

Quite naturally, however, the consideration of the basis for the dissolution of an infidel marriage in favor of the faith involves the question of the immediate origin of the Pauline Privilege. By far the more common opinion has been that Christ immediately instituted the Privilege and that St. Paul only promulgated it.[28] St. Paul's words, "For the rest I speak, not the Lord," favor the opinion that the privilege is only of mediately divine origin. But those who hold the opinion that the privilege is of immediately divine origin cite an exegesis which refers these words not to verse fifteen, which mentions

[25] De Smet, *De Sponsalibus et Matrimonio*, n. 333, 355; Cappello, *De Matrimonio*, n. 791.

[26] Bouscaren, *Canon Law Digest*, I, 552-553; the *Normae* issued by the Sacred Congregation of the Holy Office, May 1, 1934, indicated that other dissolutions of this kind have been granted and that the Helena Case was not an extraordinary and isolated case.

[27] Noldin-Schmitt, *Summa Theologiae Moralis* (3 vols., Vol. I, *De Principiis*, [32. ed. Oeniponte-Lipsiae: Rauch, 1938]), I. n. 235 et seq.; Creusen, "Baptême Douteux et Mariage Indissoluble,"—*NRT*, LII (1925), 237; Arendt, "Nota circa canonem 1127,"—*ETL*, I (1924), p. 180, n. 20.

[28] Sanchez, *De Matrimonio*, lib. VII, disp. LXXIV, n. 4; Benedict XIV, *De Synodo Dioecesana*, lib. VI, c. IV, n. 3; Perrone, *De Matrimonio Christiano Libri Tres* (3 vol., Romae, 1858), lib. II, sect. I, cap. VII, art. I; Feije, *De Impedimentis et Dispensationibus Matrimonialibus*, 9 vols., n. 471; Pesch, *Praelectiones Dogmaticae* (3 ed., 9 vols., Frisburgi-Brisgoviae, 1909), vol. VII, *De Sacramentis*, pars II, *De Matrimonio*, VII, n. 790; Wernz, *Ius Matrimoniale*, n. 702; Billot, *De Ecclesiae Sacramentis Commentarium in Tertiam Partem S. Thomae* (6. ed., 2 vols., Romae, 1922), II, 429; Wernz-Vidal, *Ius Matrimoniale*, n. 631, p. 751, note 56.

this privilege for converts, but to the preceding verses.[29] Two instructions of the Holy Office favor the opinion which regards the privilege to be of immediately divine origin.[30]

Those who hold that St. Paul both instituted and promulgated the privilege bearing his name refer the words, "For the rest I speak, not the Lord," to verse fifteen which grants the privilege, and consider them as indicative of the source of the privilege.[31] Those who support this opinion maintain that this interpretation does not destroy the necessary divine basis of the privilege and that it is more in harmony with Christ's plan of leaving to the Church a wide spiritual authority. For, as Vermeersch points out, the only positive laws which Christ laid down in the New Testament were the necessary precepts of faith and the sacraments.[32]

If St. Paul instituted and promulgated this privilege, he made use of the apostolic authority granted to St. Peter in the power of the keys, which authority was shared, of course, by St. Paul. In this way there is no need to postulate the direct intervention of Christ in the dissolution of marriage, for the argument bases on the same apostolic authority the power used by St. Paul and that used by the Popes in dissolving marriage.[33] Since, as De Smet says, the Church, of itself, has more than sufficient power, there is no apparent reason for the intervention of an immediately divine power

[29] Cornelius a Lapide, *Commentaria in Scripturam Sacrom* (Parisiis, 1866), XVIII, 306; Palmieri, *Tractatus de Matrimonio Christiano* (Romae, 1880), p. 216.

[30] S.C.S. Off., instr. (pro Vic. Ap. ad Gallas), 20 iun. 1866—*Fontes*, n. 994; S.C.S. Off., instr. (Natal), 11 iul. 1866, ad 8—*Fontes*, n. 996; cf. Wernz, *Ius Matrimoniale*, n. 702, nota. 60.

[31] Cornely, *Commentarium in S. Pauli Apostoli Epistolas*, II, *Prior Epistola ad Corinthios* (2. ed., Parisiis, 1909), p. 181; Lehmkuhl, *Theologia Moralis* (5. ed., 2 vols., Friburgi-Brisgoviae, 1888), II, n. 709; Vermeersch, *De Casu Apostoli*, n. 2; De Smet, *De Sponsalibus et Matrimonio*, n. 341; Gasparri, *Tractatus Canonicus de Matrimonio* (ed., nova ad mentem Codicis Iuris Canonici, Romae: Typis Polyglottis Vaticanis, 1932), n. 1166; Cappello, *De Matrimonio*, n. 767.

[32] *De Casu Apostoli*, n. 2.

[33] Cappello, *De Matrimonio*, n. 767.

in the case of the Apostle.[34] The question is one of fact. There is no way in which it can be settled definitively. No matter which opinion is followed, it will make no difference in the use of the privilege as such.[35]

The Pauline Privilege, however, is a species within the generic privilege of the faith. The object of an inquiry into the basis for the dissolution of marriages either certainly or doubtfully contracted in infidelity is to determine the source of the power employed in the application of the privilege of the faith. To base the Pauline Privilege upon the apostolic authority, and so to consider its origin only mediately divine, would not be to identify it with the privilege of the faith. The immediately divine origin of the Pauline Privilege could be maintained without the exclusion of another divine grant of power to solve difficulties which come under the limits of the privilege of the faith, although they are definitely outside the limits of the Pauline Privilege. The opinion favoring the mediately divine origin of the privilege affords a more logical basis for the wider privilege of the faith. Some consideration, therefore, must be given to the exact source of the power used in those cases which do not come under the Pauline Privilege.

It is by divine law that all marriages are intrinsically indissoluble. Neither the unbaptized nor the baptized can, of their own authority, withdraw their consent and so end their marriage. Yet, as is evident, not all marriages are extrinsically indissoluble, for under certain conditions the Church may dissolve the bond of marriage. The indissolubility even of infidel marriages has its foundation in the precepts of the natural law.[36]

Now, the precepts of the natural law are of two kinds, absolute and hypothetical, that is to say, conditional. The absolute precepts bind every human being; no conceivable circumstance can release anyone from the obligation to obey them. The conditional or hypothetical precepts oblige only after the human will intervenes. They do not bind until the human will has placed the act which gives rise

[34] *De Sponsalibus et Matrimonio*, n. 341.

[35] Payen, *De Matrimonio in Missionibus*, II, n. 2210.

[36] Gasparri, *Trastatus Canonicus de Matrimonio*, n. 1126.

to the obligation. Among these is the obligation to observe the indissolubility of the marriage contract.

But it happens that, because of the imprudence and thoughtlessness which sometimes mark human conduct, obligations so assumed become a positive detriment to the salvation of certain individuals. So it is that the Pope may, for a just cause, permit that the act of the will be changed or retracted and that the obligation incurred cease for this individual. This, of course, is not strictly a dispensation, that is, a relaxation of the law in a particular case, for the natural law cannot be changed even by divine power, unless human nature first be changed.[37] It is, rather, a declaration made by the Pope that, because of the urgent reasons in the case, God Himself consents to this change of will. That is to say, God uses the Church to release the individual from his obligation; and the Church acts only with vicarious power in the name of God.

In addition to the power which the Church exercises as the principal cause, she has been granted a fulness of power which she exercises in God's name as an instrumental or ministerial cause. Christ first confided these powers to St. Peter when He said to him: "And I will give to thee the keys of the kingdom of Heaven; and whatever thou shalt bind upon earth, it shall be bound also in heaven. And whatsoever thou shalt loose upon earth, it shall be loosed also in heaven." [38] And then to all the Apostles: "Amen I say to you, whatsoever you shall bind upon earth shall be bound also in heaven; and whatsoever you shall loose upon earth shall be loosed also in heaven." [39]

This unrestricted power of loosing, granted to the Church in the person of St. Peter and his successors, the Church interprets as inclusive of the vicarious power of dispensing from obligations which derive from the precepts of the natural law, once they have been freely assumed by an act of the will. This is the basis for dis-

[37] Suarez, *Opera Omnia* (ed. C. Berton, 28 vols., Parisiis, 1856-1878), Vols. V et VI, *Tractatus de Legibus*, lib. II, c. XV, nn. 16-19, 26-28; Noldin-Schmitt, *Summa Theologiae Moralis*, I, nn. 116-117.

[38] Matt., XVI: 19.

[39] Matt., XVIII: 18.

pensations, improperly so called, from vows made to Almighty God. It is also the basis for the dissolution of the bond of marriage, as effected by Paul III, St. Pius V and Gregory XIII. As Vicars of Christ, in the fulness of their apostolic authority, the popes grant for a weighty and grave cause, a dissolution of marriage contracted and even consummated in infidelity.[40]

To act validly in using this ministerial or vicarious power, which fundamentally was given to him for the salvation of souls, the Pope must have a just cause. Now the Pauline Privilege itself, as a concession in favor of the faith, clearly proves that the bond of infidel marriage can be relaxed in view of so great a good as conversion to the faith or perseverance in it. The same motive which moved St. Paul to make his grant constitutes, so it appears, a just cause for the exercise of the plenitude of apostolic authority vested in the Popes. To this authority are to be attributed the dispensations granted by the Popes in the constitutions of canon 1125; to it also is to be attributed the dissolution of the natural bond of marriage as granted by Pius XI; and to it is to be attributed the principle contained in canon 1127. For this is the ultimate basis, the intrinsic reason and the dogmatic foundation of canon 1127.[41]

[40] Billot, *De Sacramentis*, II, 434, 435; cf. Vromant, *Ius Matrimoniale* (1. ed. 1931), n. 271: "Iuris divini saltem mediate est privilegium fidei etiam late dictum; ac propterea potestas Romani Pontificis in hanc materiam dicenda est instrumentalis, ministerialis seu vicaria, atque exercetur nomine et auctoriate Christi."

[41] Arendt, "Nota circa canonem 1127,"—*ETL*, I (1924), 180-184; Hürth, "Annotationes in Decretum Sancti Officii, die 10 iunii 1937,"—*Periodica*, XXXVI (1937, 473; V. Jelicic, "De Privilegio Fidei Eiusque Fundamento Iuridico,"—*Jus Pontificium*, XVII (1937), 150.

Chapter VII

AUTHORITY GOVERNING MARRIAGE OF THE UNBAPTIZED

Before entering into a discussion of the practical application of canon 1127 to marriage in infidelity, one must necessarily review briefly the teaching of the Church in relation to the external authority competent to legislate for such marriages. The first consideration which arises when there is question of dissolving a marriage bond in favor of the faith is whether or not the marriage needs to be dissolved. Canon 1127 has no place unless it is impossible to reach moral certitude about the validity or invalidity of the marriage. It is necessary, therefore, to state briefly the nature and source of those impediments which affect the unbaptized.

Article I. Impediments of Natural and Positive Divine Law

Leo XIII [1] has pointed out that marriage, even among those who have not been baptized, is something which by its very nature is sacred and necessarily governed by law. In relation to such marriages a study will show that they are governed by the natural and positive divine law as determined by the Church, and the prescriptions laid down by the supreme civil power.[2]

The natural law evidently is binding on all men, the baptized and the unbaptized alike. The prescriptions and prohibitions of the natural law govern marriage among the unbaptized, for the tendency to marriage, because of its primary end which is the propagation of the human race through the procreation and education of children and because of its secondary end which is the mutual aid and companionship which belong to the married state, is a fundamental characteristic of human nature. Any marriage, therefore, which is contracted in violation of the natural law is not a valid marriage.

Purely ecclesiastical law, such as those laws of the Code which establish ecclesiastical impediments to marriage, do not of course bind those who are not subject to the Church by baptism.[3] But those laws

[1] Ep. encycl. "*Arcanum*"—10 febr. 1880—*Fontes*, n. 580.

[2] Payen, *De Matrimonio in Missionibus*, n. 190.

[3] I Cor., V: 12; Gasparri, *De Matrimonio*, n. 240.

of the Church which declare and determine the natural or positive divine law in relation to impediments which render marriage invalid bind even the unbaptized, for in thus declaring the divine law the Church is but carrying out her mission to preserve divine teaching intact for all men, inasmuch as all men are subject to the teaching power of the Church. Only the Church can authoritatively declare the dictates of divine law, whether that law be the natural or the positive divine law.[4]

The unbaptized, therefore, no less than the baptized, are subject to the prescriptions of the natural and positive divine law regarding the essential properties of marriage, namely, unity and indissolubility. There can be no doubt that the unbaptized must in such a manner observe the unity of marriage that the marriage of infidels is invalid unless it be the union of one man with one woman.[5] The same is true of the indissolubility of the marriage bond among infidels, for from positive divine law, all marriages are intrinsically indissoluble.[6] Indeed, such marriages, if both parties remain in infidelity, are intrinsically indissoluble, for the primary end of marriage, and consequently the good order of society, demand the stability of the marital union which otherwise would be jeopardized.

The natural law would render invalid also a marriage between two unbaptized parties if they attempted to enter marriage at an age when it would be impossible for them to have sufficient discretion to give true matrimonial consent. They would not, of course, be bound by the impediment as it is set down in canon 1067, § 1.[7]

Similarly, as canon 1068 clearly indicates, there can be no question that the diriment impediment of impotence would by the natural law invalidate a union attempted by the unbaptized if that impediment were present according to the notion indicated in ecclesiastical law. For the marriage contract consists essentially in giving and re-

[4] Canon 1038 § 1; De Smet, *De Sponsalibus et Matrimonio*, n. 426.

[5] S.C.S. Off., instr. (ad Vic. Ap. Gallas), 28 mart. 1860—*Fontes*, n. 957; S.C.S. Off., instr. (pro Vic. Ap. ad Gallas), 20 iun. 1866—*Fontes*, n. 994: Payen, *De Matrimonio in Missionibus*, n. 91.

[6] Gen., II, 23, 24; Matt., V: 31, 32; Matt., XIX: 3-9; Mark, X: 2-12; Luke, XVI: 18; I Cor., VII: 10, 11.

[7] Cappello, *De Matrimonio*, nn. 335-336; Gasparri, *De Matrimonio*, n. 497.

ceiving the right of performing those acts which of themselves are suited to the procreation of offspring. Those who are impotent cannot fulfill the essential object of the matrimonial contract.[8]

The impediment of an existing prior bond of valid marriage, founded as it is in the essential properties of marriage, also is binding on the unbaptized, for this impediment is one of the divine natural and certainly of the positive divine law. Among infidels also, the first wife and she alone is to be considered the true wife, unless, upon some other ground, the invalidity of the first union may be proved.[9] Relative to the impediment of prior bond canon 1069, § 1, makes due provision for the application of the privilege of the faith. Certainly, this impediment needs little comment; if it were not binding on the unbaptized, there would be no need of the privilege of the faith to dissolve the bond of legitimate marriage.

By far the most difficult impediment to determine in its relation to the marriage bond among the unbaptized is that of consanguinity, which is understood as a relationship by blood between two persons, due to the descent of one from the other or of both from a common ancestor. It is generally admitted that the impediment of consanguinity is founded on the natural law and that the first degree of the direct line is a diriment impediment of natural law. From this point on, the unanimity of opinion closes and the further extent of the invalidating force of the natural law becomes the subject of extensive controversy. The first degree of the collateral line is the chief object of this controversy.[10]

Since the question is of interest here only in its relation to canon 1127, it does not seem to be necessary to review the arguments employed by theologians and canonists to support varying views. These can be found at length in any commentary. This much is certain,

[8] Cappello, *De Matrimonio*, n. 347; Payen, *De Matrimonio in Missionibus*, n. 1001.

[9] Payen, *De Matrimonio in Missionibus*, n. 1047; Cappello, *De Matrimonio*, n. 390; S.C.S. Off., instr. (ad Vic. Ap. Gallas)—28 mart. 1860—*Fontes*, n. 957.

[10] Wahl, *The Matrimonial Impediment of Consanguinity and Affinity*, The Catholic University of America Canon Law Studies, n. 90, (Washington, D. C.: The Catholic University of America, 1934), p. 29.

namely, that the impediment of consanguinity in the second and third degree of the collateral line is of ecclesiastical origin only, and, therefore, does not bind the unbaptized.[11]

It is impossible to settle the controversy in relation to the invalidating force of the impediment of consanguinity in the first degree of the collateral line by any appeal to the dictates of the natural law. This question, of course, can be of practical importance in marriages contracted by the unbaptized. Upon their conversion some decision must be reached about the state of their marriages. In practice, if there is a civil law or legitimate custom invalidating such marriages, the parties are to be separated after baptism.[12] But in the absence of such a law or custom, there is at least a probable opinion that those who entered such a marriage before their conversion may remain in possession of it afterwards.[13] Cappello [14] insists that this may not be done unless the Holy See so declares and Payen [15] agrees that this is by far the safer opinion. But in virtue of canon 1127 it is certain that if one or both parties should be converted (always prescinding from the possibility of a new consummation of the marriage after the baptism of both parties), such a marriage may be dissolved in favor of the faith without recourse to the Holy See and without the making of the usual interpellations. Since there is an insoluble doubt of law inasfar as the natural law alone comes into play, regarding the validity of the marriages of persons related within controverted degrees, the privilege of the faith is in favor of the converted party or parties and the decision should favor their freedom.[16] If, as a matter of fact, those who are related within the controverted degrees had married while they were unbaptized, but later separated and contracted new marriages, there would be nothing to

[11] Cappello, *De Matrimonio*, n. 520; Payen, *De Matrimonio in Missionibus*, n. 1451.

[12] Payen, *De Matrimonio in Missionibus*, n. 1448.

[13] Gasparri, *De Matrimonio*, nn. 220, 708, 711.

[14] *De Matrimonio*, n. 521.

[15] *De Matrimonio in Missionibus*, n. 1470.

[16] Payen, *De Matrimonio in Missionibus*, n. 1448; n. 1472; Gasparri, *De Matrimonio*, n. 220; n. 711; Cappello, *De Matrimonio*, n. 521; De Smet, *De Sponsalibus et Matrimonio*, n. 355.

hinder their conversion or the recognition of these marriages by the Church. Such a situation represents an ideal example of the application of canon 1127.

From the fact that the unbaptized are bound to preserve the unity and indissolubility of the marriage bond it follows that they are bound also to give true matrimonial consent. For the unbaptized, as for the baptized, any condition or intention irreconcilable with the essential object of marriage renders the marriage invalid.[17] Likewise, if no true consent is given, then it follows from the law of nature that there is no marriage. This gives rise to a discussion as to whether or not force and fear invalidate a marriage by ecclesiastical or by natural law. There is no question here of physical violence which forces external compliance with the will of the one who exercises such violence; for the natural law invalidates any act so performed. Nor is there question of a fear so intense that it destroys the use of reason, for here again the natural law certainly invalidates any contract entered under such circumstances.[18]

Rather, the question to be considered is whether or not, independently of ecclesiastical or civil law, there is any prescript of the natural law which invalidates all marriages of the baptized and of the unbaptized which are contracted under a grave external fear that is unjustly caused to compel an exchange of matrimonial consent. Canonists are divided on this issue. The more probable view is that there is such a prescript of the natural law; the more common view is that there is not. Those who hold the affirmative opinion do so because of the very nature of the marriage contract, which demands the fullest freedom.[19] Those who deny the existence of such a prescript of the natural law do so because of the inconvenience and difficulties which would arise were its existence to be assumed.[20]

[17] Vromant, *Ius Matrimoniale* (1. ed. 1931), nn. 174-186; De Becker, *De Matrimonio*, pp. 118-128; Cappello, *De Matrimonio*, n. 574.

[18] Cappello, *De Matrimonio*, n. 606; n. 609; De Becker, *De Matrimonio*, p. 113.

[19] Payen, *De Matrimonio in Missionibus*, n. 1689; Vlaming, *Praelectiones*, I, n. 540; Cappello, *De Matrimonio*, n. 609; Cerato, *Matrimonium*, n. 83.

[20] Gasparri, *De Matrimonio*, n. 935; Vermeersch-Creusen, *Epitome*, II, n. 376; Feije, *De Impedimentis et Dispensationibus*, n. 138; Chelodi, *Ius Matri-*

Because of the probability of the opinion which affirms the invalidity of marriages contracted under the influence of force and fear even by the unbaptized, under the natural law, it is safe to say that in regard to this obstacle to true consent there is a doubt of law. Therefore, since such marriages are probably null, even if it be insolubly doubtful whether or not the fear was grave or light, upon the conversion of one or both parties to the faith, such a marriage may be dissolved in favor of the faith by applying canon 1127.[21] Unless future authentic declaration by the Holy See declares otherwise, no recourse to the Holy See is necessary in such cases.

This brief consideration of the natural and positive divine law in relation to the marriage of the unbaptized must be supplemented with a consideration of another source of diriment impediments to such marriages—those, namely, which are established by the civil authority.

Article II. Impediments of Civil Law

Since the Church makes no attempt to bind the unbaptized by her matrimonial legislation when they marry among themselves, such marriages necessarily remain under the divine law and are inherently governed by it exclusively; but they are incidentally subject also to the legislation established by the civil law. It is certain that the natural law needs much determination in relation to concrete issues. Such determination in the case of the unbaptized, if it is to exist at all, must come from the civil authority, which, outside the Church, is the only perfect society.

Until late in the eighteenth century the legislative power of the State over marriages of the unbaptized was generally admitted by canonists and theologians. No distinction was made between marriage

moniale, n. 120; De Smet, *De Sponsalibus et Matrimonio*, n. 535; De Becker, *De Matrimonio*, p. 117.

[21] Cappello, *De Matrimonio*, n. 610; Payen, *De Matrimonio in Missionibus*, n. 1690; Vromant, *Ius Matrimoniale* (1. ed.) n. 193; Knecht, *Handbuch des katholischen Eherechts* (Herder: Freiburg im Breisgau, 1928), p. 579. The Rota mentioned the principle that in doubtful matters judgment should be in favor of the faith in deciding a case of force and fear: S.R.R., *Nullitas Matrimonii*, 10 maii 1918, coram R.P.D. Gulielmo Sebastianelli, dec. V,—*Decisiones*, X (1926), 36.

and any other contract.[22] But some adopted the extreme view that such a determination of the civil law bound even the baptized. They maintained that there could be no sacrament if there was no valid contract.[23] This position, of course, represented an extreme. In refuting it some authors reached the opposite extreme by denying to the civil authority the power to regulate the marriage contract even for the upbaptized.[24] This opinion is now regarded as erroneous and it is certain that the civil authority has the right to regulate the marriage contract of the unbaptized when made among themselves, and therefore to establish not only prohibitory impediments but diriment impediments and other disqualifying laws as well.

Surely there is nothing about the nature of marriage which renders the intervention of human positive legislation odious or unreasonable. The sacramental nature of the marriage contract, when it is entered by the baptized, places Christian marriage exclusively under the jurisdiction of the Church. But marriage among the unbaptized has much in common with Christian marriage. Both are governed by the natural and positive divine law; both are contracts dependent on a true matrimonial consent for their valid existence. The welfare of society demands that there be some authority to determine more specifically what the natural law leaves undetermined. Certainly the Church has extended and clarified the natural law for the baptized, and has introduced diriment impediments which are of purely ecclesiastical law. Such legislation is necessary also for the unbaptized, and it is only reasonable that the civil authority should be able to enact just and reasonable laws, even invalidating laws, which the protection of marriage and the common good of society demands.[25]

[22] Schmalzgrueber, *Ius Ecclesiasticum Universum*, lib. IV, tit. 1, n. 364; Sanchez, *De Matrimonio*, lib. VIII, disp. III, n. 5; Wernz-Vidal, *Ius Matrimoniale*, n. 68; Payen, *De Matrimonio in Missionibus*, n. 204.

[23] Giovine, *De Dispensationibus Matrimonialibus* (2 vols., Neapoli, 1863-66) I, 124.

[24] For an account of the controversy consult Feije, *De Impedimentis et Dispensationibus Matrimonialibus*, pp. 46-48; Gasparri, *De Matrimonio*, nn. 240-242.

[25] Gasparri, *De Matrimonio*, nn. 240-246; Cappello, *De Matrimonio*, nn. 75-78; Payen, *De Matrimonio in Missionibus*, nn. 204-207; Wernz-Vidal, *Ius Matrimoniale*, nn. 67-69.

Further, from documents issued by the Holy See it seems clear that the Church concedes to the civil power the right to establish diriment impediments to marriage among the unbaptized. In an instruction issued October 29, 1739, the Supreme Congregation of the Holy Office upheld the validity of a marriage contracted in infidelity when the solemnities generally demanded by law or legitimate custom for the validity of marriage had been observed. The argument that the marriage in question would have been invalid had such solemnities been omitted, implied the right of the civil authority to establish laws affecting the validity of infidel marriage.[26]

Another response of the same Congregation regarding an infidel, who before his conversion had married his deceased brother's wife despite the existence of a diriment impediment according to the civil law, enjoined a renewal of consent after the granted dispensation from the impediment of disparity of worship and affinity. This certainly appears to indicate that the Sacred Congregation considered the marriage invalid because of the civil law impediment.[27]

The same conclusion must be drawn from an instruction issued by the Sacred Congregation for the Propagation of the Faith in regard to the faculty of dispensing polygamists. This instruction clearly recognized the power of the civil law to establish diriment impediments, for it demanded that a polygamist upon his conversion had to dismiss all of his wives except the first, unless his marriage with her had been invalid because of an impediment of the natural law or of some positive law established by their ruler.[28]

In conclusion it must be noted that missionaries working in places where such situations frequently arise regard as valid the marriages contracted according to the laws established for valid marriage by civil authority, and as invalid the marriages which when contracted

[26] Cappello, *De Matrimonio*, n. 76; Gasparri, *De Matrimonio*, n. 245.

[27] S.C.S. Off. (Yunnan), 20 sept. 1854—*Fontes*, n. 928; Cappello, *De Matrimonio*, n. 76, p. 89; Gasparri, *De Matrimonio*, n. 245.

[28] S.C.P.F., 5 dec., 1631—*Collect. S.C.P.F.*, n. 71: Gasparri, *De Matrimonio*, n. 246; Cappello, *De Matrimonio*, n. 76, p. 90.

violate such laws. This practice is well established, and as such it must have at least the tacit approval of the Holy See.[29]

[29] Cappello, *De Matrimonio*, n. 76; Gasparri, *De Matrimonio*, n. 243; Payen, *De Matrimonio in Missionibus*, n. 207; Wernz-Vidal, *Ius Matrimoniale*, n. 73.

CHAPTER VIII

PRACTICAL APPLICATION OF CANON 1127

ARTICLE I. DOUBTFUL EXISTENCE OR DOUBTFUL VALIDITY OF MARRIAGE CONTRACTED IN INFIDELITY

It is scarcely necessary to note that the privilege of the faith is a concession whereby a marriage validly contracted by two unbaptized parties may be dissolved. If the marriage has been entered invalidly, evidently it is impossible to dissolve a bond which does not exist; there is need rather for a declaration of nullity. But experience proves that it is extremely difficult to judge the validity of such marriages. It is a decision which demands diligent investigation in individual cases. Especially is this true of the status of a prospective convert who has contracted several unions.[1]

Despite the most careful investigation, however, it frequently happens that knowledge concerning the objective validity or invalidity of such marriages is obscured by insoluble doubt. But since the bond of a marriage contracted in infidelity is capable of dissolution through the exercise of the supreme ministerial power of the Pope, and since there is no danger of infringing on the absolute indissolubility of the bond of a consummated sacramental marriage, the Holy See has manifested its disposition to admit the use of the privilege of the faith in doubtful matters. Especially is this true if the doubt affects either the existence or the validity of a marriage contracted in infidelity, and if the solution of that doubt must be undertaken with a view to paving the way for the prospective reception of baptism by at least one of the parties of that marriage. The use of the privilege under these conditions was sanctioned in the former law and it obtains also in the present law of the Code according to the unanimous opinion of the canonists.

In the former law it was the constant practice of the Holy Office to permit ordinaries to consider such doubtful marriages as valid

[1] S.C.S. Off. (Siouxormen.), 18 maii 1892, ad 1, 2,—*Fontes*, n. 1155; Payen, *De Matrimonio in Missionibus*, n. 2231.

or invalid according as the favor of the faith was at stake.[2] In these responses, it is extremely difficult and of little practical moment to attempt to distinguish between the fact of marriage and its validity. From the context both possibilities are included, and the Holy Office does not, as a rule, make a sharp distinction. One conclusion is clearly evident: the Holy Office certainly applied the principle now embodied in canon 1127 to the doubtful existence or validity of infidel marriage. Canonists who wrote before the Code so understood and interpreted these responses, some of which they quoted in their entirety.[3]

That canon 1127 applies to a doubt concerning either the fact or the validity of a marriage contracted in infidelity is evident in the law of the Code. The legislation has so applied the principle that in doubtful matters the privilege of the faith enjoys the favor of the law. It is the one exception made to the general presumption which stands in favor of marriage according to the rule of canon 1014. Since the relationship of canon 1014 to canon 1127 has already been discussed, it suffices here to indicate that this specific application of canon 1127 to canon 1014, as made in the law itself, is the juridical foundation of the unanimity with which commentators so apply it.[4]

[2] S.C.S. Off., 8 iun. 1836—*Fontes*, n. 874; S.C.S. Off., instr. (ad Vic. Ap. Oceaniae Centra.), 18 dec. 1872—*Fontes*, n. 1024; S.C.S. Off., instr. (ad Ep. S. Alberti), 9 dec. 1874, nn. 12-15—*Fontes*, n. 1036; S.C.S. Off. (Mongoliae), 29 nov. 1882—*Fontes*, n. 1075; S.C.S. Off. (ad Vic. Ap. Iaponiae Merid.), 4 febr. 1891—*Fontes*, n. 1130; S.C.S. Off. (Siouxormen.), 18 maii 1892, ad 2—*Fontes*, 1155; S.C.S. Off., 18 maii 1892, ad 1—*Fontes*, n. 1156; S.C.S. Off. (Niger), 17 aug. 1898—*Fontes*, n. 1205.

[3] Wernz, *Ius Matrimoniale*, n. 702, nota 66; Gasparri, *Tractatus Canonicus de Matrimonio* (1904), n. 21; Ballerini-Palmieri, *Opus Theologicum Morale* (2. ed., 7 vols., Prati 1888-1892), Vol. VI, *De Matrimonio*, p. 352; Zitelli, *De Dispensationibus Matrimonialibus* (Romae, 1884), p. 112; De Becker, *De Sponsalibus et Matrimonio* (Bruxellis, 1896), p. 414; Feije, *De Impedimentis et Dispensationibus Matrimonialibus*, p. 338.

[4] Payen, *De Matrimonio in Missionibus*, nn. 163 sq.; 395 sq.; 1699; 2233, 2415; Vromant, *Ius Matrimoniale*, (2. ed.), n. 374; Cappello, *De Matrimonio* n. 788; Gasparri, *De Matrimonio*, n. 1168; De Smet, *De Sponsalibus et Matrimonio*, n. 355.

A. *The Investigation of the Validity of Infidel Marriage*

When the question arises as to the validity of a marriage subject to dissolution by the use of canon 1127, it is an unvarying and essential rule that before the investigating authority may arrive at a conclusion that such a marriage is invalid, or seriously and positively doubtful, he must make a careful investigation in each case. This rule has been stressed by the Holy Office in every instruction which permitted a doubtful marriage to be judged according as the favor of the faith may have suggested.[5] These instructions, indeed, not only insisted on the necessity of such an investigation; they also established clearly the principles which were to be employed in the solution of these extremely difficult cases.

In regard to marriages contracted in infidelity, even if polygamy be customary, the ruling presumption is that true marriage obtains, and not simply concubinage or a mere mating "after the manner of beasts."[6] For even in regions where concubinage is the custom it is generally true that but one woman is regarded as a true wife, she being the one first chosen.[7] But especially in mission countries priority in time does not always indicate that the first woman chosen is taken as a true wife; she who is taken in a special ceremony is the true wife who is accepted as having a special place and dignity by local custom.[8]

The presumption that true marriage is intended receives confirmation in those places where for the most part true marriages are contracted and where the fact that some kind of matrimonial union was really entered is readily demonstrable. This, of course, is true of the United States. And even if the fact of marriage appears

[5] S.C.S. Off., instr. (ad Vic. Ap. Oceaniae Central.), 18 dec. 1872—*Fnotes*, n. 1024; S.C.S. Off., instr. (ad Ep. S. Alberti), 9 dec. 1874, nn. 11, 16 et 17—*Fontes*, 1036; S.C.S. Off., instr. (ad Ep. Nesquallien.), 24 ian 1877—*Fontes*, 1050.

[6] S.C.S. Off., instr. (ad Vic. Ap. Oceaniae Central.) 18 dec. 1872—*Fontes*, n. 1024; S.C.S. Off., instr. (ad Vic. Ap. Gallas) 28 mart. 1860, n. 3—*Fontes*, n. 957.

[7] See footnote 6.

[8] S.C.S. Off., instr. (ad Vic. Ap. Gallas) 28 mart. 1860, n. 4—*Fontes* n. 957.

doubtful, the union is to be considered as a true marriage if it can be demonstrated that such a union had the appearance of a true marriage; that the woman considered herself as married legitimately; that the man treated her as his wife; and, finally, that their cohabitation was not the cause of scandal.[9] This provision may be of importance in arriving at a decision concerning the validity of the so-called common law marriage in those states where such marriages are not expressly rendered null and void by statute law.

The presumption that true marriage is intended may be weakened if in a particular region not matrimony but a kind of temporary or experimental union is contracted by the great majority. This does not mean that the presumption militates against he validity of any one particular marriage. Special investigation must disclose the exact nature of the consent exchanged before any conclusion is reached. For it is not certain and much less is it proved that even the most degenerate tribes of savages have no idea of the distinction between true marriage and concubinage. On the contrary, there is evidence that such distinctions are made.[10]

B. *The Subject Matter of Investigation*

In the light of the general principle that true marriage and not concubinage is to be presumed, the investigation of the validity of infidel marriage will center on those impediments which could render such a marriage invalid. The nature of the consent originally exchanged must be carefully investigated, for this, as experience has demonstrated, will often be the most difficult question to answer definitely.

The impediments which could render marriage among the unbaptized invalid, as determined in the preceding chapter, are the diriment impediments of the natural or the positive law and the diriment impediments of the civil law. Great care, of course, must be exercised with reference to the impediments enacted by the civil law. Accurate

[9] S.C.S. Off., instr. (ad Vic. Ap. Oceaniae Central.) 18 dec. 1872—*Fontes*, n. 1024.

[10] S.C.S. Off., instr. (ad Vic. Ap. Gallas) 28 mart. 1860, n. 4—*Fontes*, n. 957.

demonstration must show that the civil authority really intended to render invalid from the beginning and not merely rescissible, a marriage which was interdicted to the parties by the prohibition of the civil law. It is impossible to enter into a detailed discussion of such impediments here; variations of law in countries, and in the United States between State and State, must be carefully weighed.[11]

The impediments of the natural or positive divine law which may invalidate marriage among the unbaptized are impotence, consanguinity in the first degree of the direct line (and very probably in any degree of the direct line and in the first degree of the collateral line.)[12] and prior bond.[13] The prior bond of a valid marriage is evidently the impediment which will obtain most frequently, as the whole subject under discussion clearly indicates. If this impediment or any other of the natural or positive divine law is *certainly* present, a marriage attempted, despite its existence, is invalid.[14]

Also subject to diligent inquiry is the nature of the consent exchanged. This investigation should be conducted according to the norms established in canons 1081-1087. For these canons, with a few minor and evident exceptions, are a clear statement of the natural law.[15] It will be necessary to discover whether there was a true matrimonial consent, truly intended and sufficiently manifested externally and, therefore, not fictitious and not substantially vitiated.[16] At times it is highly necessary to determine whether any consent was exchanged at all. This is especially true with reference to men in such places where polygamy is common.[17]

[11] Cf. Alford, *Jus Matrimoniale Comparatum* (Kenedy: New York, 1938). This work presents a thorough study of the relationship of American civil law to the matrimonial law of the Code.

[12] Cf. canons 1068; 1076.

[13] Canon 1069.

[14] Payen, *De Matrimonio in Missionibus*, n. 2234; Vromant, *Ius Matrimoniale* (1. ed. 1931), n. 374; Léry, *Le Privilège de la Foi*, pp. 36-40; "Commentaire du Canon 1127,"—*L'Ami du Clergé* XLII (1925), 220-223.

[15] Payen, *De Matrimonio in Missionibus*, n. 2234.

[16] Vromant, *Ius Matrimoniale* (1. ed., 1931), nn. 174-186; Payen, *De Matrimonio in Missionibus*, nn. 2234-2235.

[17] S.C.S. Off. (Victoriae Nyanzae), 3 apr. 1889.—*Fontes*, n. 1115; S.C.S. Off. (Coreae), 12 sept. 1855—*Fontes*, n. 934.

If consent was truly given, investigation should be made to discover whether it may have been vitiated by fear (which is very probably according to the dictate of the natural law itself an obstacle to the validity of marriage) or by the positive exclusion of one of the essential properties of marriage,[18] or by the presence of some condition which militates against a substantial element of the matrimonial contract, such as its perpetuity or indissolubility.[19]

If after careful investigation there is serious doubt about the validity of a marriage contracted by an infidel, especially in regions where temporary unions are frequent, the oath of the infidel that he has never contracted an indissoluble union with any of his former wives may be accepted to complete the proof of his freedom.[20] However, Payen [21] clearly indicates his distrust in the reliability of an oath taken by converts in China, and Vromant [22] extends this observation to include all neophytes. Practical experience demonstrates the wisdom of this attitude. Furthermore, for the completion of proof this oath could be accepted only when likely evidence concerning the nullity of the marriage has been gathered from other sources to such a measure that its corroboration by means of the oath will become a practical equivalent of conclusive proof.[23]

Finally, if an impediment of the positive divine law has disappeared, for example the impediment of prior bond through the death of the former legitimate spouse, it must be remembered that the exant marriage of two unbaptized consorts, the status of which was invalid prior to the cessation of the impediment, becomes convalidated with the cessation of the impediment apart from any formal renewal of their matrimonial consent.[24]

If at the time that a marital union was entered, either or both

[18] Canon 1086 § 2.

[19] Canon 1092; S.C.S. Off., instr. (ad Vic. Ap. Oceaniae Central.), 6 apr. 1843—*Fontes*, n. 894; S.C.S. Off., instr. (ad Ep. Nesquallien.), 24 ian. 1877—*Fontes*, n. 1050.

[20] S.C.S. Off. (Siouxormen), 18 maii 1892, ad 1.—*Fontes*, 1155.

[21] *De Matrimonio in Missionibus*, n. 2234.

[22] *Ius Matrimoniale* (1. ed. 1931), n. 186.

[23] Vermeersch, *De Casu Apostoli*, n. 21.

[24] Canon 1133, § 2. Alford, *Jus Matrimoniale Comparatum*, p.

parties did not give true matrimonial consent, because the marriage was intended to be temporary or entirely experimental in character, then such a marriage was certainly invalid. Regularly, however, it should be considered as validated by the supervening consent, if the union endures for a long period of time and circumstances indicate that the defective consent has been rectified.[25]

C. *The Application of Canon 1127 to Dubious Marriages*

If the investigation conducted according to the norms established by the Holy Office terminates in the conclusion that a marriage of two unbaptized parties is only probably invalid, then the circumstances of the case under discussion will determine the nature of the judgment to be rendered.[26] In some instances the parties of such a doubtful union will be most anxious to validate their marriage. If both parties are converted, such validation should take place after their baptism. They must observe the canonical form in the renewal of their consent. Should any impediment of ecclesiastical law be present, then a dispensation should be granted after their baptism and before their renewal of consent.[27]

If only one party is converted and wishes to continue marital life with a pagan partner who has no wish to be baptized, then the renewal of consent should take place before baptism in order to safeguard the convert's right to use the Pauline Privilege in case future events should make this necessary. Since the validation itself is uncertain, the necessity of exacting the formal guarantees[28] cannot be urged with absolute rigor and insistence. But the danger of perversion must be removed and the convert must be disposed to educate all of the children of the union in the Catholic faith.[29] Evidently this

[25] S.C.S. Off. (Siam), 22 nov. 1871—*Fontes*, n. 1019. S.C.S. Off., instr. (ad Ep. S. Alberti), 9 dec. 1874—*Fontes*, n. 1036.

[26] Payen, *De Matrimonio in Missionibus*, n. 2333; Vromant, *Ius Matrimoniale* (1. ed., 1931), n. 285; Léry, *Le Privilège de la Foi*, n. 31; Cappello, *De Matrimonio*, n. 788.

[27] Vromant, *Ius Matrimoniale* (2. ed., 1938), n. 375.

[28] Canon 1071.

[29] S.C.S. Off., instr. (ad Vic. Ap. Oceaniae Central.), 18 dec. 1872—*Fontes*, n. 1024; S.C.S. Off., instr. (ad Ep. S. Alberti), 9 dec. 1874—*Fontes*, n. 1036; cf. Vromant, *Ius Matrimoniale* (2. ed., 1938), n. 375.

procedure cannot always be followed. It would apply especially and almost exclusively to a marriage of two unbaptized partners neither of whom had been previously married, but whose matrimonial consent was doubtful.

Quite frequently the convalidation of marriages relative to which the validity is subject to prudent well-founded doubt cannot be effected. Separation of the parties in such a marriage may be equally impossible. In such cases it was the practice of the Holy Office to allow a convert in favor of the faith, to remain in possession of his or her marriage. In two instructions this doctrine is expressed in clear and unmistakable terms.[30] It was the decision of the Holy Office that such marriages were to be considered valid even when "there was place neither for a separation nor, because of the malice of the unbaptized party, for a renewal of consent." For "it is too evident to need repetition that in such circumstances the favor of the faith demands that these marriages be judged as valid."[31] Thus in the case of an insoluble doubt as to the validity of a marriage contracted in infidelity the decision should favor the faith. If considering the marriage as valid will open the way to conversion and the reception of baptism, the doubtful marriage should, in favor of the faith, be held as valid.[32] It must be borne in mind that at least from the woman's viewpoint in such cases a separation from her consort would be a heavy burden, one that in many cases would be an obstacle to her conversion.

On the other hand, the favor of the faith in the great majority of cases will demand that doubtful marriages be judged as invalid to

[30] S.C.S. Off., instr. (ad Vic. Ap. Oceaniae Central.), 18 dec. 1872—*Fontes*, n. 1024; S.C.S. Off., instr. (ad Ep. S. Alberti), 9 dec. 1874, nn. 12-15—*Fontes*, n. 1036.

[31] S.C.S. Off., instr. (ad Ep. S. Alberti), 9 dec. 1874, ad 12-13: "Cum vero causa in incerto relinquitur, et neque separationi sit locus, neque ex malitia partis infidelis consensus renovationi, item qui petit Baptismum est baptizandus, id que duplici ex ratione: 'In re dubia in favorem fidei pronunciandum esse constans regula est; ait Benedictus XIV; iam vero clarius est quam ut dici oporteat, in his adiunctis favorem fidei postulare ut stetur pro matrimonii validitate"—*Fontes*, 1036.

[32] Payen, *De Matrimonio in Missionibus*, n. 2233; Vromant, *Ius Matrimoniale* (2. ed., 1938), n. 375.

establish the freedom of a prospective convert to enter a new marriage with a Catholic. Whenever this obtains, then a marriage which is not certainly invalid should, in favor of the faith, be considered null. The numerous instructions of the Holy Office so frequently cited here all support this conclusion. These responses affect not only a polygamist when none of his marriages is certainly valid, but also those men and women who were doubtfully married to only one consort.[33] The responses may be summarized as follows: "If one party alone is converted to the faith, the other remaining in infidelity, the Holy Father is to be requested to grant the Vicar Aposolic faculties to dispense the convert from the interpellations. But if one party is converted after the conversion of the other and, after a careful examination of each case, there is still doubt (as to validity), then in favor of the faith the marriage is to be considered null.[34] It may be noted here that even if both parties are converted at the *same* time, there is no reason for the solution of the case to differ. There is no essenial difference between such a hypothesis and the case solved by the Holy Office. The favor of the faith could be extended.[35]

The Holy Office also issued a response to settle difficulties caused by polygamous marriages. "If, after careful examination, the marriage with the first wife who is already baptized is found to be valid, the convert polygamist is bound to return to her. If she is not baptized, it will be sufficient to interpellate her concerning her possible desire of conversion. If she is unwilling to become converted, or if there is serious doubt as to the validity of the marriage with the first wife, the converted polygamist may marry any of the women whom he will, provided first that she become baptized and thereupon renew her consent." [36] The principle upon which these documents are based is that the judgment in a doubtful case should be in favor of the faith. It is a principle which is often implied and repeatedly also expressed.[37]

[33] S.C.S. Off. (Siouxormen.), 18 maii 1892—*Fontes*, n. 1*55; S.C.S. Off. (Zanguebar), 18 maii 1892, ad I—*Fontes*, n. 1156.

[34] S.C.S. Off. (Zanguebar) 18 maii 1892, ad I—*Fontes*, n. 1156.

[35] Payen, *De Matrimonio in Missionibus*, nn. 165; 2333.

[36] S.C.S. Off. (Siouxormen.), 18 maii 1892, ad 2—*Fontes*, n. 1155.

[37] Payen, *De Matrimonio in Missionibus*, nn. 2233; 163; 395; 1699.

D. *The Concession in Practice*

The examination of a marriage contracted in infidelity may be instituted by means of a procedure of an extrajudicial summary character. There is no need to use the solemnities of a formal trial to determine whether or not the doubt requisite for the use of canon 1127 is present.[38] Payen maintains that the right to judge regarding the existence of the requisite doubt belongs to the ordinary [39] by delegation of the Holy See.[40] He also holds that in mission countries all missionaries may likewise be considered as delegates of the Holy See, under the authority of the ordinary.[41]

Vromant holds that there is no need to seek the intervention of the local ordinary or of the Holy See. The judgment is not reserved, so he contends, if the doubt is prudently considered to be present. The Holy See has by the common law authoritatively and practically settled the doubt in favor of the faith. But because of the difficulty of arriving at a safe conclusion in these serious matters, he holds that priests and missionaries, according to the norms of canons 296 and 336, § 2, are subject to the instructions and precepts of their local ordinaries.[42]

Of these two opinions Payen's appears to rest on a more secure juridical foundation, for the use of the Pauline Privilege itself and of the faculties mentioned in the constitutions of canon 1125 are subject to such regulations as the local ordinary may make. Practically the two opinions are in accord. The ordinary can, of course, appoint a delegate to act for him in this matter. Generally considered, however, a case which may be settled according to the disposition of canon 1127 will be decided by members of the diocesan tribunal, who will proceed not only as the nature of the case may

[38] Payen, *De Matrimonio in Missionibus*, n. 2333; n. 1699; Vromant, *Ius Matrimoniale* (1. ed., 1931), n. 186, nota 4; De Becker, "De Procedura Adhibenda Quoties Infidelis Matrimonium cum Parte Catholica Inire Vult" —*ETL*, I (1924), 36 sq.

[39] Cf. canon 198.

[40] *De Matrimonio in Missionibus*, n. 2233; cf. also canon 1962.

[41] *De Matrimonio in Missionibus*, n. 2233.

[42] Vromant, *Ius Matrimoniale* (2. ed., 1938), n. 372.

demand, but also in accordance with the instructions which the local ordinary may see fit to give.

There remains the question as to the necessity of obtaining a dispensation from the interpellations if a doubtful marriage is considered as invalid. Payen's conclusion is that neither the interpellations nor a dispensation from them can be said to be strictly necessary. Yet, he concludes, that practically it is better always to ask for a dispensation *ad cautelam.*[43] Vromant holds that the interpellations may be omitted inasmuch as the right of the infidel consort is at most still an uncertain right.[44]

Payen points out, however, that in two responses the Holy Office directed that a dispensation from the interpellations be given even though the marriages in question were of but doubtful validity.[45] Another response cited by Payen demanded that formal interpellations be made though the marriage was doubtful because of doubtful consent. However, this case evidently was to be settled by the use of the Pauline Privilege in its strict sense. The response does not seem to offer conclusive proof that it was the mind of the Holy See to demand either the interpellations or a dispensation from them when a marriage contracted in infidelity was positively doubtful.[46]

Wernz[47] and De Smet[48] support Vromant's view that the great majority of the responses of the Holy Office make no such demand; that the infidel party has no strict right in such a case and that any advantage that may be gained by the application of canon 1127 would be lost if the interpellations had to be made. But it may be noted that the doubtful validity of such marriages would offer a sufficient reason for a dispensation from the interpellations.[49]

[43] *De Matrimonio in Missionibus*, nn. 2233, 2240-2244.

[44] *Ius Matrimoniale*, (2. ed., 1938), n. 369; S.C.S. Off., instr. (ad Ep. S. Alberti), 9 dec. 1874, ad 13—*Fontes*, n. 1036; S.C.S. Off. (Siouxormen.), 18 maii 1892—*Fontes*, n. 1155.

[45] S.C.S. Off. (Zanguebar), 18 maii 1892, ad 1—*Fontes*, n. 1156; S.C.S. Off., 16 aug. 1894—*ASS*, XXIX, (1894) 565.

[46] S.C.S. Off., 26 apr. 1899—*Fontes*, 1222.

[47] *Ius Matrimoniale*, n. 705, nota 92.

[48] *De Sponsalibus et Matrimonio*, n. 355.

[49] Gregory, *The Pauline Privilege*, pp. 78-79; Cappello, *De Matrimonio*, n. 781.

However, the opinion which eliminates the need of the interpellations or of any dispensation from them seems to be the better one if the purpose and the effect of the application of canon 1127 are kept in mind.

Article II. Canon 1127 in Relation to Certain and Doubtful Baptism

For the purpose of accuracy it was thought better in the preceding article to confine the discussion to the application of canon 1127 to marriages of but doubtful validity contracted by those who certainly have never been baptized. The present article is a treatment of cases in which the fact of baptism, whether of certain or doubtful validity, has intervened.

A. *Marriages between the Unbaptized and Certainly Baptized Heretics*

At the outset it must be stated that, contrary to what seems to be a widespread misconception, canon 1127 cannot be applied in the case of a marriage contracted by a party who is certainly unbaptized with one who is certainly baptized in heresy. It is presumed, of course, that the marriage was contracted after the Code had gone into effect. In such a case the foundation for the application of canon 1127 is entirely absent. There is no question of doubt; the validity of the marriage in question as well as the baptism of one party is certain.[50]

Such a marriage is capable of dissolution by the use of the privilege of the faith in virtue of canon 1125. But in the present discipline the Holy Office has reserved to itself exclusively the judgment of such cases. No local ordinary is now, or in the past ever was, competent to grant the dissolution of the natural bond of marriage under such circumstances. This does not necessarily mean that the Holy See may not employ the principle of canon 1127 in determining whether or not it is expedient to dissolve a particular marriage con-

[50] Vromant, *Ius Matrimoniale* (2. ed., 1938), nn. 369; 379.

tracted under such circumstances, but that again is a judgment exclusively reserved to the Holy See.[51]

B. *Doubtfully Valid Use of the Pauline Privilege*

There is no question that the Pauline Privilege is a concession "in favor of the faith." [52] But there is great difficulty as to the interpretation of that term. For this reason there exists a controversy as to the capacity of those who join a christian denomination by the valid reception of baptism for using this privilege. The majority of canonists hold the position that the privilege is attached to the sacrament of baptism, and that, herefore, all who are converted from infidelity and are validly baptized, whether in the Catholic Church or in a non-catholic sect, may use it.[53]

There are not lacking, however, authors of great repute who hold the view that St. Paul's words [54] must be construed in such a way that the foundation of the Pauline Privilege is not alone the valid reception of baptism but the profession of the Catholic faith as well. They support their view by quoting the words of Innocent III, "si enim alter infidelium coniugum ad fidem catholicam convertatur," as definite proof that the true faith is essential to the use of the privilege.[55] Gasparri maintains that this question was presented for solution to the Holy Father in 1859 (Pius IX) but that he was unwilling to settle the dispute. The question is therefore still an open

[51] Cf. Vromant, *op. cit.*, n. 379; Bouscaren, *Canon Law Digest*, I, 552, 553; II, 157; "Dispensation from natural marriage 'in favorem fidei'—An important decision"—*ER*, LXXII (1925), 186-188.

[52] Canon 1120.

[53] Ballerini-Palmieri, *Opus Theologicum Morale*, VI, 457; Fahrhner, *Geschichte des Unauflöslichkeitsprinzips und der vollkommenen Scheidung der Ehe im kanonischen Recht* (Freiburg im Breisgau, 1903), p. 290; De Smet, *De Sponsalibus et Matrimonio*, n. 345; Wernz-Vidal, *Ius Matrimoniale*, n. 601; Chelodi,*Ius Matrimoniale*, n. 157 cum notis; Cappello, *De Matrimonio*, n. 769; Vermeersch-Creusen, *Epitome*, II, n. 428; Payen, *De Matrimonio in Missionibus*, n. 2253.

[54] I Cor., VII: 12-14.

[55] Rosset, *De Sacramento Matrimonii* (6 vols., Parisiis, 1895-1896) I, n. 616; cf. ep. *Quanto te magis*, 1 maii 1199—c. 7, X, *de divortiis*, IV, 19.

one and complete freedom of opinion as to its answer is allowed. Gasparri supports the doctrine that the Pauline Privilege may not be so applied is certain.[56] Vlaming[57] supports Gasparri's teaching and Vromant also considers this negative opinion as solidly probable.[58]

If, therefore, a marriage contracted in infidelity is considered to have been dissolved through the use of the Pauline Privilege, invoked by a former infidel now validly baptized in an heretical or schismatic sect, such a dissolution, and also the second marriage contracted on the strength of it, may be considered a doubtful matter. For, even granted that the heretical baptism was valid, that the interpellations were made, and that the second union was contracted with a woman also validly baptized in heresy, such a use of the Pauline Privilege is only a probably valid use. The validity of the second marriage is correspondingly only a probable validity. As far as this writer is able to determine, Vromant is the only author who has considered this possible use of the Pauline Privilege in relation to canon 1127.[59] However, one must read the context carefully to avoid misunderstanding Vromant's treatment of the question. In n. 374 of the work here cited he seems to be of the opinion that, upon the conversion of one or both parties of the second marriage to the Catholic faith, this second marriage may in virtue of canon 1127 be considered valid or invalid according as the favor of the faith may be at stake.[60]

It is safe to say that the validity of the second marriage could be rendered certain by the application of canon 1127. If the baptisms of the parties are doubtfully valid, baptism may be conferred upon them conditionally even subsequent to their conversion to the faith. The consent should be renewed, and the marriage should be rendered certain by the dissolution of the former bond which may be effected through the use of the privilege of the faith which in this doubtful

[56] *De Matrimonio*, n. 1136.

[57] *Praelectiones*, n. 720, nota 3.

[58] "Haeretici et schismatici, etsi baptizati, privilegio Paulino probabiliter valide uti nequeunt"—*Ius Matrimoniale* (2. ed., 1938), n. 284.

[59] *Ius Matrimoniale* (2. ed., 1938), n. 374 and n. 378; Cappello (*De Matrimonio*, n. 788) makes what may be considered a very confused reference to this problem.

[60] Vromant, *op. cit.*, nn. 374-375.

matter enjoys the favor of the law. In this case no recourse to the Holy Office is necessary. The local ordinary can act on his own authority.

But it is obvious that canon 1127 could never be used to *dissolve* the second marriage, i. e., the marriage contracted by the probably baptized parties. The bond of the former marriage contracted in infidelity may still exist or it may not. The question as to the valid use of the Pauline Privilege by non-Catholics is still open. Both partners of the second marriage are either certainly or doubtfully baptized. If, therefore, this second marriage has been consummated (which is presumed by law) it is, to say the least, a doubtfully contracted sacramental union which has become consummated. Canon 1127 is of no avail under such circumstances; the Holy Father would never risk the dissolution of a sacramental marriage which has become consummated, for such a marriage is indissoluble except by the death of one of the partners.[61] It should be noted, however, that Payen[62] is of the opinion that such a case should be referred to the Holy See for a decision. To illustrate the point at issue, he cites a case in which Cornelius, a Jew, married Iphigenia, an infidel. After a civil divorce, Cornelius became an Episcopalian and after having interpellated Iphigenia in vain, entered a union with Lucy, who was also an Episcopalian. Some years later Iphigenia was converted to the Catholic faith and thereafter both Cornelius and Lucy wished to be received into the Church. Payen advises that the question as to whether or not they may be received into the Church without being made to separate should be referred to the Holy See. Obviously the Catholic baptism of Iphigenia in the case proposed by Payen is a complicating factor. It seems to be a necessary conclusion that the solution of such a case must be left to the Holy See. Had Iphigenia never been baptized, canon 1127 would be applicable to effect the certain dissolution of Cornelius' marriage with her. But in view of the many difficulties that may arise in such cases, Payen's advice is sound, and in practice by far the safer course to pursue.[63]

[61] Canon 1118; cf. Vromant, *Ius Matrimoniale* (2. ed., 1938), n. 378; Vromant, "Le Privilège de Foi au Canon 1127,"—*NRT*, LIX (1932), 449.

[62] *De Matrimonio in Missionibus*, n. 2253.

[63] *De Matrimonio in Missionibus*, n. 2253.

C. The Use of the Pauline Privilege by the Doubtfully Baptized

1. NORMS RELATIVE TO THE VALIDITY OF BAPTISM

Fundamental to the validity of baptism is the use of the proper matter and form and the presence of the necessary intention of the minister of the sacrament. The matter of baptism may be divided into remote and proximate.[64] The remote matter, determined by Christ Himself, is natural water: "Unless a man be born again of *water* and the Holy Ghost, he cannot enter the kingdom of God."[65] The proximate matter is the ablution or the washing which, for validity, may be done by infusion, immersion or aspersion.[66] The essential element seems to be the ablution which takes place when the water flows upon the skin of the head of the person to be baptized. For the Holy Office ordered the conditional repetition of baptism conferred by an unction instead of an ablution.[67] The form of the sacrament necessary for validity is the expression of the baptismal action in the name of one God in three divine persons: "*Ego te baptizo in nomine Patris et Filii et Spiritus Sancti.*" The matter and form of the sacrament must be morally united.

These elements are essential. To omit either of them would render the baptism invalid. Doubt of the validity of baptism may, therefore, center about the matter and form used in its administration. But, in addition, there is required the intention of the minister.[68] Especially in relation to canon 1127, much discussion has arisen concerning the intention required of the minister of baptism.[69]

64 Cf. Schenk, *The Matrimonial Impediments of Mixed Religion and Disparity of Cult*, pp. 119-147; S. C. de Prop. Fide, instr. (ad Vic. Ap. Siam), 23 iun. 1830—*Coll. S.C.P.F.*, n. 814; *Fontes*, n. 4748.

65 John, III: 5; Denzinger-Bannwart, Enchiridion, n. 858; canon 737, § 1.

66 Canon 758.

67 S.C.S. Off., 14 dec. 1898—*Fontes*, n. 1211.

68 Conc. Trident., sess. VII, *de sacramentis in genere*, can. 11—Denzinger-Bannwart, *Enchiridion*, n. 854.

69 A discussion concerning the presumed invalidity of non-Catholic baptisms in the United States was carried on between Joseph P. Donovan, C.M., and Valentine Schaaf, O.F.M., in a series of articles published in *The Ecclesiastical Review*. Cf. *ER*, LXXIV (1926), 158-180; LXXV (1926), 131-151

Beginning in the very early centuries of Christianity, the problem of determining the validity of baptism has engaged the mind of the Church and of her theologians and canonists. This anxiety centered particularly on the validity of baptism conferred outside the Catholic Church and, in a special way, on the intention of those who administered the sacrament. Obviously it is neither necessary nor possible to trace either the historical development of this problem or its solution. The controversies among the theologians did not serve to give a satisfactory answer whereby the presence of the required internal intention of the minister could be determined. The great scholastics approached the solution when they taught that the minister of baptism is the rational instrument of Christ and of the Church and that he, therefore, must have the intention to do what they do.[70] This statement concerning the nature of the intention required of course did not obviate the difficulty of determining whether or not the intention, which is internal and hidden, was truly present. St. Thomas Aquinas in answering this difficulty pointed out that the minister of the sacrament acts in the person of the whole Church, whose minister he is; the intention which he expresses in the words which he pronounces is that of the whole Church and this intention is sufficient for the validity of the sacrament unless it is openly contradicted by the minister of the sacrament or by the recipient.[71]

The Council of Trent required of the minister the intention of doing what the Church does.[72] The Council did not demand for validity that this intention be expressed or determined; it required only the general intention of doing what the Church does, what Christ instituted or what Christians do.[73] To allay all disquietude

and 358-370; LXXVI (1927), 155-165 and 496-504; LXXXIV (1931), 124-139 and 282-295 and 371-387; see also Bouscaren, *Gregorianum*, VIII (1927), 41-54.

[70] Petrus Lombardus, *Petri Lombardi Libri IV Sententiarum* (studio et cura PP. Collegii S. Bonaventurae in lucem editi, 2. ed., 2 vols.; Ad Claras Aquas [Quarrachi] 1916), Sent. Lib. IV, Dist. VI, cap V.

[71] *Summa Theologica*, IIIa, q. 64, art. 8 ad 2.

[72] Sess. VII, *de sacramentis in genere*, can. 11—Denzinger-Bannwart, *Enchiridion*, n. 854.

[73] S.C.S. Off., instr. (ad Custodem Terrae Sanctae), 30 ian. 1833—*Fontes*, n. 871.

and anxiety over the presence of the required intention, the Church herself established the principle that the needed intention of the minister was to be presumed if there was at hand evidence of the proper administration of the matter and form of the sacrament.[74]

It is significant that the principle thus established was primarily an answer to questions which arose in relation to the validity of non-Catholic baptisms. And it must be borne in mind that the intention to do what a sect does is sufficient to constitute a general intention of doing what the universal Church does.[75] Moreover, the Council of Trent [76] did not require the intention of doing what the Church intends; it required for validity only the intention of doing what the Church *does*. For this reason errors about the nature of baptism or of its efficacy can be reconciled with the intention of doing what the Church does.[77] The fact that the minister expressly tells a candidate that baptism will have no effect on his soul does not necessarily and of itself demonstrate the invalidity of the baptism conferred as the result of a lack of the necessary intention.[78] The Church is concerned primarily with the integrity of the rite of baptism. When the proper matter and form have been employed, the needed intention is to be presumed as being present. For by its very nature the intention is internal and hidden and the rule established by the Church is the only one that effectually precludes anxieties and scrupulosity.[79]

It is well known, of course, that certain sects repudiate baptism.

[74] S. C. de Prop. Fide, instr. (ad Vic. Ap. Siam), 23 iun. 1830—*Coll. S.C.P.F.*, n. 814; *Fontes*, n. 4748.

[75] Bellarminus, *Opera Omnia ex Editione Veneta* (iterum edidit Justinus Fevre, 12 vols., Parisiis, 1870-1874), lib. I, *de sacramentis in genere*, cap. XXVII—Tom. III, 413.

[76] Sess. VII, *de baptismo*, canon 4—Denzinger-Bannwart, *Enchiridion*, n. 860.

[77] S.C.S. Off., instr. (ad Ep. Nesquallien.), 24 ian. 1877—*Fontes*, n. 1050; S.C.S. Off., instr. (ad Custodem Terrae Sanctae), 30 ian. 1833—*Fontes*, n. 871; S.C.S. Off., instr. (ad Vic. Ap. Oceaniae Central.), 18 dec. 1872—*Fontes*, n. 1024.

[78] S.C.S. Off., instr. (ad Vic. Ap. Oceaniae Central.), 18 dec. 1872—*Fontes*, n. 1024.

[79] S.C.S. Off., instr. (ad Custodem Terrae Sanctae), 30 ian. 1833—*Fontes*, n. 871.

Thus the Quakers and the Socinians have always rejected baptism and do not administer it.[80] The Methodists, however, have varied their practice. In 1845 the Congregation for the Propagation of the Faith mentioned baptisms conferred by them as being initially presumed to be doubtful, for at that time the Methodists denied the necessity of baptism and usually rejected the rite.[81] But in an instruction sent to the bishop of Nesqually (Seattle), the Holy Office admitted no such presumption of suspicion because the Methodists were, as a matter of fact, again administering baptism. The bishop's contention, namely, that the change from the former practice of not administering baptism did not remove the doubt, was rejected by the Holy Office.[82]

Only those baptisms, therefore, which are conferred in sects which repudiate baptism are initially presumed to be of doubtful validity. When, as a matter of fact, a sect does prescribe baptism, its ritual must first be examined before any presumption is formed. If the ritual prescribes a valid matter and form, the baptism so conferred will be initially presumed to be valid. If the rite prescribed is of doubtful validity, or of manifest and evident invalidity, the presumption will bear the corresponding character.

The value of this initial presumption must not be overestimated. The investigation of the validity of baptism cannot be allowed to stop at this presumption. Each case must be examined individually. The norm of this investigation established by the Holy Office centered on two points: 1. "*Utrum ritus administrandi sacramentum Baptismi ab ista secta in istis regionibus retentus, aliquid contineat quod illius nullitatem inducere valeat.* 2. *Utrum talis sectae ministri de facto sese conforment praescriptionibus in propria eorum secta sanctis.*" The ritual of the sect and the actual administration of baptism by the minister represent the scope of the investigation. But in addition the intention of the minister must also be investigated.[83]

80 S.C.S. Off., instr. (ad Ep. Nesquallien.), 24 ian. 1877—*Fontes*, n. 1050.

81 S. C. de Prop. Fide, instr. (ad Vic. Ap. Pondicher.), 26 iul. 1845—*Fontes*, n. 4815.

82 S.C.S. Off., instr. (ad Ep. Nesquallien.), 24 ian. 1877—*Fontes*, n. 1050.

83 S.C.S. Off. (Bulgariae), 5 iul. 1853—*Fontes*, n. 925.

Such an investigation may prove that the minister acually did not have the proper intention or it may at least present a positive indication that the intention was of doubtful validity. If no such indications are disclosed, the necessary intention of doing what the Church does, or what Christ commanded, is to be presumed if the proper matter and form have been employed. It is, of course, needless to repeat that the Holy See has insisted constantly on the necessity of careful examination into each particular case.[84]

In conclusion, before a baptism is judged as certainly valid, or as certainly invalid, or as of insolubly doubtful validity, the following norms must be employed: 1. a baptism which is initially presumed to be valid must be considered valid until a positive reason is found for regarding it as invalid or of insolubly doubtful validity; 2. a baptism which is initially presumed to be doubtful must be considered doubtful until a positive reason is disclosed which points to manifest validity or invalidity; 3. a baptism initially presumed to be invalid is to be so regarded until the presumption of invalidity is compelled by prevailing positive reasons to yield to a presumption of doubt or validity.

It frequently happens in individual cases, when there is some evidence for the fact of baptism, that for various reasons such baptisms cannot be examined in the light of an initial presumption. The conclusion to be reached in these cases will depend on the evidence discovered in the individual investigation. As long as evidence is wanting to produce moral certainty either for the fact of its administration or for the use of a valid rite, this lack of evidence forms a positive reason for regarding the baptism as doubtful.

Direct proof of baptism may be acquired through witnesses[85] or through documents.[86] But, in relation to the use of canon 1127, indirect proof through presumptions will be far more often employed whether the point to be proved be the very fact that baptism was

[84] S.C.S. Off. (Bulgariae), 5 iul. 1853—*Fontes*, n. 925; S.C.S. Off., instr. (ad Ep. Nesquallien.), 24 ian. 1877—*Fontes*, n. 1050; S.C.S. Off., instr. (ad Vic. Ap. Iaponiae Merid.), 4 febr. 1891—*Fontes*, n. 1130.

[85] Canon 742, § 1; 779.

[86] Canons 1813-1816; 1990.

ever administered, or whether, if it was administered, that the baptism was valid. For, as practical experience amply demonstrates, it is no easy matter to obtain baptismal certificates from many non-Catholic sects, nor is their authenticity and probative value always above serious reproach.[87] Thus, if there is evidence for the fact of the administration of baptism, the decree of the Holy Office dated November 17, 1830, will serve as a guide in attaining moral certainty of the validity or invalidity of the baptism.[88] If doubt arise as to the very fact of the administration of baptism, the decision of the Holy Office sent to Bishop Gross of Savannah[89] will serve as a reliable guide.[90] The statement of these principles was deemed necessary as an introduction to the treatment of the applicability of canon 1127 in allowing the use of the Pauline Privilege to those whose baptisms are of doubtful validity. If it is possible to arrive at moral certainty as to the validity or the invalidity of such baptisms, then it is the mind of the Holy See that meticulous examination shall omit no factor which may clarify the issue. When, therefore, the term "doubtful baptism" is employed in reference to canon 1127, there is understood such a doubt which, despite careful examination in the individual case, is found to be morally insoluble. This usage of the term is essential to a proper understanding of the decree of the Holy Office which was issued on June 10, 1937.[91]

2. THE 1937 DECREE OF THE HOLY OFFICE ON DOUBTFUL BAPTISM

In countries such as the United States, where civil divorce laws are lax and where protestantism is predominant, the importance of determining whether doubtful baptism may be included among doubtful matters in the sense of that term as employed in canon 1127 is evident. Among many of these non-Catholic sects the very fact of the administration of baptism, or the validity of the baptism (if

[87] Cappello, *De Matrimonio*, n. 420.

[88] S.C.S. Off., 17 nov. 1830—*Fontes*, n. 869; Cappello, *De Matrimonio*, n. 421.

[89] S.C.S. Off. (Savannah), 1 aug. 1883—*Fontes*, n. 1083.

[90] Cappello, *De Matrimonio*, n. 421; Vromant, *Ius Matrimoniale* (1. ed., 1931), nn. 78, 79; 284.

[91] AAS, XXIX (1937), 305-306.

conferred), may readily remain a matter of insoluble doubt. Experience proves that many vexing problems may arise upon the conversion of non-Catholics who wish to marry Catholics. Canonists were not slow to realize the purpose which canon 1127 might serve were it to be applied to dissolve the bond of marriages contracted by non-Catholics, one or both of whose baptisms were of insolubly doubtful validity. Indeed, the doubt connected with this question was proposed to the Holy Office for authoritative solution, and in 1937 the following document was issued:

Suprema Sacra Congregatio S. Officii
Decretum 10 iunii 1937

In plenario conventu huius Supremae Sacrae Congregationis Sancti Officii, habito Feria IV, die 5 maii 1937, propositis dubiis:

1. Utrum in matrimonio contracto a duobus acatholicis dubie baptizatis, in casu dubii insolubilis circa Baptismum possit permitti altrutri parti ad Fidem conversae usus Privilegii Paulini vi can. 1127 Codicis Iuris Canonici?

2. Utrum in matrimonio contracto interpartem nonbaptizatum et partem acatholicam dubie baptizatum, in casu dubii insolubilis de Baptismo, possint Ordinarii alterutri parti ad Fidem Catholicam conversae permittere usum Privilegii Paulini vi can. 1127?

Emi ac Revmi Dñi Cardinales Fidei morumque integritati tutandae praepositi, omnibus mature perpensis, respondendum decreverunt:

Ad 1. Negative.

Ad 2. Recurrendum ad S. Officium in singulis casibus. Hanc vero emorum Patrum resolutionem, in audientia E.P.D. Adsessori S. Officii die 13 eiusdem mensis et anni impertita, SSmus D. N. Pius Divina Providentia Pp. XI adprobare et Suprema Sua Auctoritate confirmare dignatus est, ac publici iuris fieri iussit:

Datum Romae, ex Aedibus S. Officii, die 10 iunii 1937.

I. Venturi, Supremae S. Congr. S. Officii Notarius.

a. Doubtful Baptism of Both Parties

Certainly it is not surprising that the Holy Office refused to allow the use of canon 1127 to effect the dissolution of a marriage contracted by two parties both of whose baptisms are of insolubly doubtful validity. Such usage of the Pauline Privilege was denied by the Holy Office in a response given before the Code. The case concerned the doubtful validity of the baptisms received by both parties. One of the partners refused to live peacefully with the other who had been received into the Church. Because of a very grave doubt concerning his previous baptism, it was asked whether the convert might be considered as a convert from infidelity and by the application of the Pauline Privilege be permitted to contract a new marriage. The answer of the Holy Office denied the use of the Pauline Privilege under such circumstances.[92]

The reply of the Holy Office given in 1937 is a definitive solution; the principle of canon 1127 cannot be applied either to consider the two doubtful baptisms null (thus permitting the application of the Pauline Privilege) or to employ the Pontifical power to dissolve the first matrimonial bond in view of the doubt about its sacramental nature. Creusen[93] maintained that the Holy Office gave the same reply in a particular case after Pentecost, 1918. No canonist who wrote before the promulgation of the Code expressed the opinion that the marriage of two doubtfully baptized partners could be dissolved in favor of the faith. The presumption of the validity of baptism "*in ordine ad validitatem matrimonii*" would have upheld the sacramental nature of such a bond. Of those who have considered the problem in relation to canon 1127, only a very few held

[92] "Utrum pars conversa propter gravissimum dubium de baptismo in haeresi recepto aequiparari possit parti ab infidelitate conversi et propter Paulinum privilegium ad alias nuptias transire?" S. C. respondit "Negative." —S.C.S. Off., instr (ad Vic. Ap. Oceaniae Central.), 18 dec. 1872, ad 2—*Fontes*, n. 1024.

[93] "Baptême Douteux et Mariage Indissoluble," *NRT*, LII (1925), 231.

clearly that such marriages were subject to dissolution in virtue of this canon.[94]

Blat, whose authority was adduced to uphold the affirmative opinion,[95] did not say that canon 1127 applied to the marriage of two doubtfully baptized parties. Nor do the decisions of the Holy Office to which he refers contemplate such a case. Vermeersch, in 1922, did hold this opinion[96] But, after reconsideration, he retracted his former view.[97] Creusen wrote at great length to demonstrate the unsoundness of the affirmative opinion,[98] and Arendt[99] strongly condemned Cerato's admission of such a use of canon 1127.

There can be no question that the great weight of canonical authority was opposed to the application of canon 1127 to matrimonial cases when the doubt in question touched the validity of the baptisms received by both parties. For, as all who have commented on this recent decree of the Holy Office point out, the theological principles involved make any other decision of the question impossible.[100] If a marriage has been contracted by two persons both of whose baptisms are doubtful, that marriage is a legitimate marriage if factually one or both of the baptisms are invalid. Such a union is dissolved only by an authority constituted by the positive divine law. If both of the baptisms are valid, then the union is a sacramental union. When such a marriage has been consummated, it be-

[94] Cerato, *Matrimonium*, n. 127; Donovan, "A New Marriage Case,"—*ER*, LXX (1924), 59-64; "Doubtful Baptisms and Pauline Privilege,"—*ER*, LXXI (1924), 48-53; "Doubtful Baptisms Again,"—*ER*, LXXII (1925), 622-628.

[95] *Commentarium*, III, pars I, n. 538.

[96] "Interpretatio Canonis 1127,"—*Peridoca*, X (1922), (27).

[97] "De Usu Privilegii Fidei in Re Dubia,"—*Periodica*, XIII (1924, 212.

[98] "Baptême Douteux et Mariage Indissoluble,"—*NRT*, LII (1925), 227-241.

[99] "Nota circa Canonem 1127,"—*ETL*, I (1924), p. 181, n. 24.

[100] Hürth, "Annotationes ad Decretum S. Officii, die 10 iunii 1937,"—*Periodica*, XXVI (1937), 473; Creusen, "Application du privilège paulin dans les cas douteux,"—*NRT*, LXIV (1937), 1123; Dalpiaz, "Annotationes ad Decretum S. C. Sancti Officii d. 10 iunii 1937,"—*Apollinaris*, X (1937), 337; Cappello, *De Matrimonio*, n. 788; Lèry, *Le Privilège de la Foi*, n. 114; Vromant, *Ius Matrimoniale* (2. ed., 1938), n. 370.

comes indissoluble; for no human authority can dissolve the bond of a sacramental consummated marriage.[101]

If the parties to such a marriage maintain that the union was not consummated, there would be place 1) for the process which is required for the purpose of establishing the nullity of the marriage in consequence of the impediment of impotence, or 2) for the process which is required for the purpose of obtaining a dispensation from the bond of a sacramental marriage which has not been consummated. In favor of the common good, or of the propagation of the true faith, the legislator may indeed establish presumptions which preclude the necessity of strict proof concerning certain facts. But such presumptions may not be employed when they would involve the danger of violation of the divine law. The Holy See, therefore, clearly refuses to allow the use of canon 1127 in the case under discussion because there would be grave danger of attempting to dissolve a consummated sacramental marriage.

The decision of the Holy Office in this case is in perfect accord with the attitude of the Holy See in analogous cases. For the Holy See requires moral certitude that the bond of one marriage does not exist before it permits a second union.[102] Thus, also, a marriage will not be allowed as long as there exists a prudent doubt which favors the possibility that the parties who wish to marry are related in any degree of the direct line of consanguinity or in the first degree of the collateral line.[103] So, too, when there is question of a marriage contracted by two doubtfully baptized partners, the use of canon 1127 is denied because of the proximate danger of violating the divine law of the absolute indissolubility of a consummated sacramental union. In consequence of the strong probability that neither the Pauline Privilege nor the wider privilege of the faith could be validly applied under such circumstances, any permission to contract a new mar-

[101] Canon 1118.

[102] Quamvis prius matrimonium sit irritum aut solutum qualibet ex causa, non ideo licet aliud contrahere, antequam de prioris nullitate aut solutione legitime et certo constiterit.—Canon 1069, § 2.

[103] Numquam matrimonium permittatur si quod subsit dubium num partes sint consanguineae in aliquo gradu lineae rectae aut in primo gradu lineae collateralis.—Canon 1076, § 3.

riage would, in effect, be a permission to contract an invalid and adulterous union. This conclusion obtains even if the doubt about the validity of a convert's former baptism is sufficiently founded to warrant the conditional administration of the sacrament when he is received into the Church. When eternal salvation is at stake the safer course must always be followed.[104]

b. Doubtful Baptism of One Party

The reply of the Holy Office to the second question submitted for solution is one of great practical importance. This question had reference to a marriage in which the non-baptism of one party is certain and the validity of the other party's baptism, conferred in a non-Catholic sect, is insolubly doubtful. The inquiry presupposed that canon 1127 could be applied to permit the use of the Pauline Privilege; it asked only if the local ordinary might authorize the use of the canon and whether a second marriage might be contracted on the strength of it.[105]

The Holy Office in its response did not deny that canon 1127 applied in this case, but it did restrict the rights of the local ordinary insofar as it reserved to itself the right to examine and adjudicate such matters. This decision may appear to be unduly strict, but those who have commented upon it [106] point out that it is the sanctity of the marriage bond and the grave danger of scandal which led the Holy Office to make this ruling. As Cappello points out,[107] this is not a definitive solution of the question asked; it is merely a practical norm of action. From the text of the response it is not at all clear that the recourse required by it is necessary for the validity of a second marriage contracted without the making of this recourse.

104 S.C.S. Off., instr. (ad Vic. Ap. Oceaniae.), 6 apr. 1843—*Fontes*, n. 894.

105 Hürth, "Annotationes ad Decretum S. Officii, die 10 iunii 1937,"—*Periodica*, XXVI (1937), 475; Creusen, "Application du privilege paulin dans les cas douteux,"—*NRT*, LXIV (1937), 1124; Dalpiaz, "Annotationes ad Decretum S. C. Sancti Officii, d. 10 iunii 1937,"—*Apollinaris*, X (1937) 337.

106 Cf. authors cited in note 105.

107 *De Matrimonio*, n. 788.

Such a case would have to be submitted to the Holy Office for a solution.

That such recourse might later be required was early foreseen by some canonists.[108] But the vast majority of writers had no hesitation in permitting the local ordinary to allow the use of canon 1127 in a case wherein only one party was doubtfully baptized and the other was certainly not baptized. No authority, of course, can be drawn from pre-Code canonists. Such a marriage in the former law would have been invalid because of the impediment of disparity of worship.[109] For, as the instructions of the Holy Office clearly indicate, in the law existing before the Code a doubtful baptism was presumed valid "*in ordine ad validitatem matrimonii.*"

This presumption, which favored the validity of the baptism even to the prejudice of the validity of the marriage, was not a mere human conjecture of validity, established solely for the practical service of determining the validity of a marriage. It was and is a presumption based on the divine law.[110] If the rite of baptism has been conferred, there is a "*presumptio iuris et de iure divino*" that the one to whom such a rite has been administered is subject to the laws of the Church. To destroy the force of this presumption it must be proved either that the rite was not conferred or that it was conferred invalidly. Therefore, when the impediment of disparity of worship affected all the baptized, it made no distinction between those who had been doubtfully and those who had been certainly baptized. It included all those who had been admitted to the jurisdiction of the Church through the sacrament of baptism as it is recognizable by the administration of the baptismal rite. The doubtfully baptized were included in the very law of the impediment.

In relation to the question at issue, the solution offered no difficulty. If the baptism was truly valid, the marriage was certainly

[108] Cf. Ayrinhac, "Pauline Privilege and Doubtful Baptism,"—*ER*, LXXIII (1925), 65-72.

[109] S.C.S. Off., 17 nov. 1830—*Fontes*, n. 869; S.C.S. Off., instr. (ad Vic. Ap. Oceaniae), 6 apr. 1843—*Fontes*, n. 894; S.C.S. Off., instr. (ad Ep. Nesquallien.), 24 ian. 1877—*Fontes*, n. 1050.

[110] Cf. Arendt, "Brevis Animadversio circa Interpretationem Doctrinalem § 2, Canonis 1070,"—*Jus Pontificium*, V (1925), 136.

invalid because of the impediment of disparity of worship. If the baptism was invalid, the principle in force before the Code, and now stated clearly and specifically in canon 1127, indicated sufficiently that it was the mind of the Holy Father to include in his permission of the use of the Pauline Privilege a dissolution of the natural bond of marriage in such cases insofar as it was necessary.[111]

This solution, of course, was rendered impossible by the change made in the extent or limit of the impediment of disparity of worship by canon 1070, § 1. A marriage contracted before Pentecost 1918 is to be judged by the law under which it was contracted. A marriage contracted after Pentecost 1918 by two parties, one of whom is certainly unbaptized and one of whom is doubtfully baptized in a non-Catholic sect, would be a valid union whether in fact the doubtful baptism is valid or invalid. For in the Code the impediment of disparity of worship affects only those who have been baptized in the Catholic Church or who have been converted to it from heresy or schism, should they attempt marriage with a person who is unbaptized. Non-Catholics have been exempted from the effects of the impediment as long as they marry among themselves.[112]

But since such marriages are not sacramental, even though the baptism of one party was certain, canonists were almost unanimous in applying the principle of canon 1127 to the marriages in which one party was doubtfully baptized in a non-Catholic sect and one party was certainly not baptized. The canonical reasoning on which this unanimity was based was unquestionably solid. The bond of legitimate marriage can be dissolved by Papal Authority for a grave reason. If the dubious baptism in the case was in reality valid, canon 1127 implied the intervention of this supreme power of the Pope. If the baptism was invalid, the Pauline Privilege dissolved the bond of the first marriage when the second union was contracted

[111] Arendt, "Nota circa Canonem 1127,"—*ETL*, I (1924), 182; Creusen, "Baptême Douteux et Mariage Indissoluble,"—*ETL*, LII (1925), 231; Dalpiaz, "Annotationes ad Decretum S.C.S. Officii, d. 10 iunii 1937,"—*Apollinaris*, X (1937), 339.

[112] Nullum est matrimonium contractum a persona non baptizata cum persona baptizata in Ecclesia catholica vel ad eandem ex haeresi aut schismate conversa.—Canon 1070, § 1.

with a Catholic. It is true that Augustine[113] denied the use of the Pauline Privilege in such a case, but he gave no reasons for so doing. Arendt also held that the Pauline Privilege was not applicable and that it was only by the direct intervention of the supreme ministerial power of the Pope that such a bond could be dissolved.[114] But such a conclusion goes farther than the decision of the Holy Office given in 1937. This decision does not say that the Pauline Privilege can not be applied; it merely reserves to the Holy See the right to decide as to the manner of solution. In following this decision (1937) of the Holy Office, the local ordinary would do well from the outset to handle such cases according to the norms laid down by the Holy Office on May 1, 1934, to obtain the dispensation "*super vinculo naturali.*" In that way all the necessary information will be at hand and the reply of the Congregation will be facilitated. Evidently there is a close parallel between two possible methods according to which the dissolution of the existing union may be effected.

In conclusion, while it is certainly safe to say that the norm of practical action as indicated by the Supreme Congregation of the Holy Office must be followed, and that any other course of action would be the height of rashness, the answer of the Holy Office on June 10, 1937, does not settle the theoretical question involved. The answer does not indicate that the principle of canon 1127 may not be applied in the case of a single doubtful baptism in order to allow the use of the Pauline Privilege. It simply restricts the right of judgment to the Holy Office alone. But the intrinsic probability of the reasoning which would permit the use of the principle enunciated in canon 1127 and consequently also the application of the Pauline Privilege, together with the extrinsic weight of canonical authority which favored such a procedure as being inherently possible, indicates that theoretically such an application of canon 1127 is juridically sound. The restriction was made to prevent every danger of laxity and abuse. Such a danger would certainly arise were canon 1127 to be used without scrupulous regard for the careful examination

[113] *A Commentary on the New Code of Canon Law* (4. ed. revised, 8 vols., S. Louis: Herder, 1918-1929), Vol. V, 368.

[114] Arendt, "Nota circa Canonem 1127,"—*ETL*, I (1924), 182-183.

which such a serious matter demands. Not a few authors, all of whom wrote before 1937, allowed the use of canon 1127 in a case wherein only one party was doubtfully baptized, the other being certainly unbaptized.[115]

c. Doubtful Baptism in the Catholic Church

The foregoing discussion was of necessity restricted to the question of the application of canon 1127 to a marriage contracted by a party who was certainly not baptized with one whose baptism in a non-Catholic sect was insolubly doubtful. It is not impossible, however, that an insoluble doubt may be present either in regard to the fact or with reference to the validity of a baptism conferred in the Catholic Church.

Surely it is a point which needs no insistence, namely, that should such a doubt concerning the baptism of a person in the Catholic Church arise before marriage is contracted, he should be rebaptized conditionally. This is true whether the doubtfully baptized person intends to marry a party who is certainly not baptized, or who is a baptized Catholic, or who is a certainly or doubtfully baptized non-Catholic. Apart from any questions concerning the validity of the marriage to be contracted, there is present also the absolute necessity of following the safer course in regard to a necessary means of salvation.[116]

The present consideration, however, concerns only the doubt regarding the fact of baptism or the validity of the baptism conferred in the Catholic Church, with relation to a person who has already contracted marriage with a person who is certainly not baptized. According to canon 1070, § 1, all those who have been baptized in

[115] Cappello, *De Matrimonio* (3. ed., Taurinonum Augustae: Marietta, 1933) n. 788; Farrugia, *De Matrimonio*, n. 326; Creusen, "Baptême Douteux et Mariage Indissoluble,"—*NRT*, LII (1925), 239; Vermeersch, "De Usu Privilegii Paulini in Re Dubia,"—*Periodica*, XIII (1924), (212); Vermeersch-Creusen, *Epitome*, n. 437; De Smet, *De Spons. et Mat.*, n. 355; Payen, *De Matrimonio in Missionibus* (2. ed. 1935-36), n. 2415 bis; Vromant, *Ius Matrimoniale* (1. ed., 1931), n. 293.

[116] Vromant, *Ius Matrimoniale* (1. ed., 1931), n. 81; Payen, *De Matrimonio in Missionibus*, n. 1113; Cappello, *De Matrimonio*, n. 418.

the Catholic Church or converted to it from heresy or schism are bound by the impediment of disparity of worship.[117] The principle that a doubtful baptism is presumed to be valid "*in ordine ad validitatem matrimonii*" is conditioned in the present law by the principle "*in dubio standum est pro valore matrimonii.*" For in canon 1070, § 2, the following norm is established:

> **si pars tempore contracti matrimonii tamquam baptizata commiter habebatur aut eius baptismus erat dubius, standum est, ad normam can. 1014, pro valore matrimonii, donec certo probetur alteram partem baptizatam esse, alteram vero non baptizatam.**

Evidently the prescriptions of canon 1070, § 2, are applicable only to those who, in accordance with paragraph one of the same canon, are bound by the impediment of disparity of worship.

Now, two hypotheses present themselves in regard to a marriage contracted between a person doubtfully baptized in the Catholic Church and a person who has never been baptized. This marriage was contracted either with or without a dispensation from the impediment of disparity of worship. If at the time of the contraction of this marriage such a dispensation had been sought and obtained, the subsequent conditional rebaptism of the putative Catholic will not allow the dissolution of such a marriage by the use of the Pauline Privilege.[118]

Vromant is of the opinion that such a marriage could be dissolved by a special indult which the Holy See could grant, but he and other authors are one in denying the application of canon 1127 to

[117] For a discussion of the meaning of the term "baptized in the Catholic Church," see Schenk, *The Matrimonial Impediments of Mixed Religion and Disparity of Cult*, nn. 158-184; Cappello, *De Matrimonio*, n. 412; Payen, *De Matrimonio in Missionibus*, n. 1097; Vromant, *Ius Matrimoniale*, (1. ed., 1931) nn. 69-76.

[118] Canon 1120; S.C.S. Off. (Cochinchin.), 1 aug. 1759, ad 4—*Fontes*, n. 810; (Nankin), 5 mart. 1852—*Fontes*, n. 918; (Siam), 4 iul. 1855—*Fontes*, n. 931; instr. (ad Ep. S. Alberti), 9 dec. 1874—*Fontes*, n. 1036.

such a case.[119] Cappello is also of the opinion that a marriage contracted with a dispensation from the impediment of disparity of worship can be dissolved by pontifical power, but he (as do all other authors) admits that this it not the practice of the Holy See.[120] Practically, therefore, canon 1127 cannot be applied to a marriage contracted with a dispensation from the impediment of disparity of worship even though the baptism of one party in the Catholic Church was doubtful.

But if such a marriage was contracted without a dispensation from disparity of worship, there seems not to be present any solid reason which prevents the local ordinary from applying canon 1127 in favor of the faith. Suppose, for example, that the unbaptized party wished upon the later reception of baptism to enter a new marriage with a Catholic, but was prevented from doing so by the uncertain bond of his former marriage. The other party's doubtful baptism in the Catholic Church was either valid or invalid. If the baptism was invalid, the marriage would be only a legitimate marriage, subject *servatis servandis* to dissolution by the use of the Pauline Privilege. If the baptism was valid, the marriage would be invalid in view of the existing impediment of disparity of worship.

The response of the Holy Office given in 1937 [121] did not consider the factor of doubtful baptism in the Catholic Church; it considered merely the doubtful baptism received in a non-Catholic sect. While canon 1070, § 2, directs that a marriage is to be considered as valid until it is certainly proved that at the time of that marriage one party was certainly baptized and the other was certainly not baptized, nevertheless it indicates that canon 1014 provides the norm of judgment. And canon 1014 expressly makes an exception in favor of canon 1127. It is true that neither Creusen,[122] nor Dalpiaz,[123] nor

[119] Vromant, *Ius Matrimoniale* (2. ed., 1938), n. 377, nota 1; De Becker, *De Sponsalibus et Matrimonio*, p. 434; De Smet, *De Sponsalibus et Matrimonio*, n. 355.

[120] *De Matrimonio*, n. 791; cf. Gasparri, *De Matrimonio*, n. 1170.

[121] AAS, XXIX (1937), 305-306.

[122] "Application du privilège paulin dans les cas douteux,"—*NRT*, LXIV (1937), 1123-1124.

[123] "Annotationes ad Decretum S.C.S. Officii,"—*Apollinaris*, X (1937), 333-339.

Hürth,[124] consider the case as it is presented here, but that does not mean that they exclude the use of canon 1127 when there is question of a baptism doubtfully conferred in the Catholic Church and when a dispensation from the impediment of disparity of worship has not intervened. Vromant states explicitly that canon 1127 may be so applied,[125] as do Léry [126] and Cappello.[127] If such a case should arise, any local ordinary would be within his rights and would act not only according to the letter but also according to the spirit of the law in permitting the use of the Pauline Privilege through the application of canon 1127 under such circumstances.

One may note in concluding this article that there is no solid juridical reason for attempting to apply canon 1127 when a serious doubt arises as to whether a dispensation from the impediment of disparity of worship was granted. The same holds true when despite the granting of a dispensation a serious doubt arises for a variety of reasons regarding the validity of the dispensation. Among such reasons the following may be recounted as examples: 1) the doubtful execution of the rescript of dispensation; 2) the absence of any notation of the granted dispensation in the marriage records; 3) the missionary's doubtful possession of faculties for granting the dispensation; and 4) the possibly or probably mistaken granting of a dispensation from the impediment of mixed religion in the case.[128]

Vromant mentions these doubts without venturing any opinion as to the application of canon 1127 to their solution.[129] Léry excludes such matters from the ambit within which the principle of canon 1127 may be applied.[130] His solution (and the writer's) implies that such cases be presented to the Holy Office for their final settlement. If the dispensation has been validly granted and applied, then canon

[124] "Annotationes ad Decretum S.C.S. Officii,"—*Periodica*, XXVI (1937), 473-475.

[125] *Ius Matrimoniale* (2. ed., 1938), n. 373.

[126] *Le Privilège de la Foi*, n. 114.

[127] "Quaestiones Peculiares," *Jus Pontificium*, XX (1940), 30; *De Matrimonio*, n. 788, *ad finem*.

[128] "Commentaire au canon 1127,"—*L'Ami du Clergè*, XLII (1925), 223.

[129] *Ius Matrimoniale* (2. ed., 1938), n. 374.

[130] *Le Privilège de la Foi*, n. 114.

1127 is definitely excluded. The Holy See alone is competent to decide such problems or to extend the favor of the law.[131]

[131] Arendt, "Nota circa canonem 1127,"—*ETL*, I (1924), p. 182, n. 30.

CHAPTER IX

CANON 1127 IN RELATION TO THE PAULINE PRIVILEGE AND THE CONSTITUTIONS OF CANON 1125

ARTICLE I. THE NECESSARY CONDITIONS FOR THE USE OF THE PAULINE PRIVILEGE

That the use of the Pauline Privilege be certainly valid, four conditions must be present. First, the marriage bond to be dissolved must have been contracted while both parties of the union were unbaptized. Secondly, one party in the conversion from infidelity must be validly baptized while the other party chooses to remain in infidelity. Thirdly, the infidel party must desert the convert, that is, the unconverted party must persevere in infidelity and refuse to continue peaceful cohabitation with the convert. Fourthly, by means of the interpellations it must be fully established that the infidel party has really departed.

Thus far, in the practical application of canon 1127, the discussion has been restricted almost exclusively to the first of these conditions. For the Pauline Privilege applies certainly only when there is a valid marriage between two certainly unbaptized partners.[1] If the doubtful existence or the doubtful validity of such a marriage rests on a solidly probable basis, then canon 1127 applies; if the infidel status of the parties is doubtful because of the doubtful baptism of one or both parties, the nature of the case will determine the applicability of canon 1127.[2]

The second condition, namely, the necessity of conversion and of the reception of a valid baptism, needs hardly to be stressed. It is a basic principle that the use of the Pauline Privilege presupposes the previous reception of a valid baptism.[3] The Holy See has declared that catechumens cannot avail themselves of the privilege, even if

[1] Canon 1120.

[2] Cf. *supra*, Chapter VIII.

[3] Canon 1121.

their infidel spouses force them to lead a life of sin or repudiate them on account of their newly-found religion.[4] And, in special reference to canon 1127, it may be stated here that the favor of the faith conceded by this canon is restricted unquestionably to the Catholic faith alone, to the absolute exclusion of any christian sect. For this canon implies the intervention of the supreme ministerial power of the Holy Father who certainly intends to favor only the Catholic religion.[5] The Holy Father cannot exercise this power except in favor of one who is certainly baptized; for obvious reasons he cannot supply certainty in relation to a doubtful baptism.[6]

But a consideration of the remaining conditions for the valid use of the Pauline Privilege indicates that they may be the source of many perplexities which offer wide possibilities for the use of the principle of canon 1127. The establishment of the departure of the unconverted spouse and the response to the interpellations have been, in the jurisprudence of the Holy Office, the occasion for the development and for the application of the principle that in doubtful matters the privilege of the faith enjoys the favor of the law. This article, then, presupposes a legitimate marriage which is certainly valid, and concerns itself only with those doubts which may arise in relation to the use of the Pauline Privilege in the strict sense of that term.

A. *Physical and Moral Departure*

The use of the Pauline Privilege is allowed to a convert if the departure of his infidel consort is either physical or moral. Actual physical desertion is realized if the unbeliever unjustly leaves a convert who has been faithful and who has given no cause for desertion. Such departure is verified if the infidel contracts marriage with another person; if he is detained by this second marriage or by creditors

[4] S. C. de Prop. Fide (ad C. P. pro Sin.—Pekin.), 16 ian. 1803, ad 1—

[5] Vromant, *Ius Matrimoniale* (2. ed., 1938), n. 369.

Coll. S.C.P.F., n. 665; *Fontes*, n. 4671; S.C.S. Off., 13 mart., 1901—ASS. XXXIII, 549-550.

[6] Vromant, *op. cit.*, n. 370.

because of unpaid debts; or if he separated out of hatred for the christian faith.[7]

Moral departure is effected by the infidel if, apart from an express refusal of physical cohabitation, his words or his actions demonstrate his refusal to cohabit peacefully. For in these circumstances the cohabitation would be such as to imperil the faith of the convert or to offer serious injury to God or to the christian religion. Concretely, this departure will be realized when the infidel refuses to give up a life of concubinage,[8] or when he denies to his offspring a Catholic education,[9] or when he attempts to lead the convert into idolatry or into any grave sin.[10]

Moral departure is also considered to have taken place if the infidel causes an unhappy married life in which severe quarrels continually arise. Presumably, of course,the convert is not the culpable cause of these difficulties.[11] Grave and incurable vices of the infidel also represent a real servitude for the convert and thus constitute a moral departure on the part of the infidel spouse.[12]

Addiction to alcohol or to drugs likewise constitutes such a departure, as does an excessive love of gambling, a life of crime or a confirmed habit of extreme laziness and cruelty. If, either by the common law or by means of a special indult, a dispensation allows that the convert be asked only if he wishes to be converted, and if his reply is affirmative though he is at the same time the slave of such vices, then despite his affirmative answer he is considered as having morally departed. For, as Payen indicates, the sincerity of

[7] S.C.S. Off. (Cochinchin.), 12 iun. 1850—*Fontes*, n. 910; S.C.S. Off. (Siam), 4 iul. 1855—*Fontes*, n. 931; cf. Gregory, *The Pauline Privilege*, p. 58.

[8] S.C.S. Off. (Siam), 4 iul. 1855—*Fontes*, n. 931; S.C.S. Off. (Natal), 11 iul. 1866, ad 2—*Fontes*, n. 996.

[9] S.C.S. Off. (Tunkin Occident.), 14 dec. 1848, ad 2—*Fontes*, n. 908; S.C.S. Off. (Natal), 11 iul. 1866 ad 4—*Fontes*, n. 996.

[10] S.C. de Prop. Fide, 5 mart. 1816, ad 6—*Coll. S.C.P.F.* n. 704.

[11] S.C.S. Off. (Cochinchin.), 1 aug. 1759, ad 2—*Fontes*, n. 810; S.C.S. Off., 26 apr. 1899—*Fontes*, n. 1222; Payen, *De Matrimonio in Missionibus*, n. 2280, 2, 3; Lèry, *De Privilège de la Foi*, n. 50.

[12] Vermeersch, *De Casu Apostoli*, n. 45.

his wish to be converted and baptized would have to be based on the hope of a miracle.[13] In the weighing of these evidences of departure on the part of the infidel, it is quite possible that doubt as to the reality of his desertion may arise. Such doubts may, in virtue of canon 1127, be settled in favor of the convert. But the use of the canon demands the greatest care in the thorough investigation of each case. For in a reply given on November 22, 1871, the Holy Office required recourse to the Holy See in each doubtful case when such evidence was submitted to it as the cause for a dispensation from the interpellations.[14] Canon 1127 indeed grants greater freedom, but in view of this response of the Holy See the greatest care and prudence must be exercised to safeguard the validity of its use.[15]

Fundamental to this notion of the departure of the infidel, whether that departure be actually a physical separation or simply a moral separation, is the perseverance of the unbaptized party in infidelity. For, if after the separation has been effected, the infidel should also be baptized before the party who was first converted has entered a new marriage, the Pauline Privilege is no longer applicable. The first marriage has become sacramental because of the baptism of both parties and is, therefore, subject to the laws of the Church governing christian marriage.[16]

Even if the baptism of one party is of but doubtful validity, canon 1127 cannot be applied. Recourse would have to be made to the Holy Office in each case.[17] But it must be noted that the convert would not lose the right to contract a new marriage if his infidel partner actually has not been baptized, even though this partner has indicated a future disposition to be baptized.[18]

[13] *De Matrimonio in Missionibus*, n. 2283.

[14] S.C.S. Off. (Siam), 22 nov. 1871, ad 2-5—*Fontes*, n. 1019.

[15] Payen, *De Matrimonio in Missionibus*, n. 2415 bis; Lèry, *Le Privilège de la Foi*, n. 51.

[16] Canons 1118, 1119.

[17] *AAS*, XXIX (1937), 305-306.

[18] S.C.S. Off. (Siam), 22 nov. 1871—*Fontes*, n. 1019; S.C.S. Off. (Victoriae Nyanzae), 8 iul. 1891, ad 1, 2, *Fontes*, n. 1040; S.C.S. Off., 26 apr. 1899—*Fontes*, n. 1222.

1. Culpable Physical Departure

Inseparably united with the perseverance of the unconverted spouse in infidelity is his refusal to cohabit peacefully without injury or insult to the Creator. If the infidel is completely opposed to continuing marital life with the convert, it is immaterial what motive has led him to arrive at this decision, provided only that the newly converted spouse did not, after baptism, furnish a cause which warranted the infidel party's separation as a righteous and reasonable procedure.[19] Thus, if after baptism, the converted party is guilty of adultery, the law forbids the use of the Pauline Privilege.[20]

In this connection there arises the possibility of an application of canon 1127. Aemilius Van Henexthoven, superior of the Jesuit Missions in Kwango (Africa), proposed a difficulty of this kind to the Holy See. After recalling that the Holy See had more than once declared that adultery and other delicts which had been committed before baptism were to be considered condoned after baptism, and that the use of the Pauline Privilege was not to be denied because of them, he asked: "What if, after baptism, the adultery or other delict be repeated, in such a way however that it is morally certain that, because the parties are separated by long distances, these delicts were not the cause of separation, since the infidel knew nothing of his partner's baptism nor of her morals thereafter, and would have refused cohabitation in any case?" In its reply, the Holy Office refused to answer directly the question whether faults committed after baptism are an obstacle to the use of the Pauline Privilege by the baptized party if they are inconsequential to the infidel or even entirely unknown to him. The Holy Office decided, in its reply, that its former decree of August 1, 1759, and an instruction of the Congregation for the Propagation of the Faith, dated January 16, 1797, be forwarded to the petitioner for his guidance and to this decision

[19] S.C.S. Off. (Cochinchin.), 1 aug. 1759, ad 2—*Fontes*. n. 810; S.C.S. Off., 26 apr. 1899—*Fontes*, n. 1222.

[20] Canon 1123; S. C. de Prop. Fide, *Fontes*, n. 4652 (ad C. P. pro Sin.), 16 ian. 1797, ad 2—*Coll. S.C.P.F.*, n. 634; *Fontes*, n. 4652.

it added the formula: *et ad mentem: mens est ut in dubiis, iudicium sit in fidei favorem.*[21]

The 1759 decree of the Holy Office indicates that the convert enjoys the favor of the faith and, therefore, for any just cause, he may use the Pauline Privilege. The 1797 instruction of the Congregation for the Propagation of the Faith demanded that the interpellations be made in a case wherein adultery committed before the baptism of the convert might have been the cause of the infidel's departure. In the instruction it was indicated that no account was to be taken of the temporal precedence of the expulsion by the infidel or of the adultery.[22]

From a study of these responses of the Holy See it is evident that the Holy Office considered the right of the convert to use the Pauline Privilege as doubtful, even though the unconverted party had no knowledge of the convert's delicts after baptism. But it is also evident that this doubt was to be resolved in favor of the faith or of the liberty of the convert. For, in the case presented, the departure of the infidel was formally sinful. Though a righteous cause for separation existed, he had no knowledge of it and it could not, therefore, be the cause of the separation.

According to the principle of canon 1127, the local ordinary could permit the use of the Pauline Privilege under the same circumstances. Arendt [23] maintains that the dissolution of the former marriage in this case should be attributed rather to the direct intervention of the supreme ministerial power of the Pope than to the Pauline Privilege. But there is a sufficient weight of extrinsic authority to make the use of the Pauline Privilege safe in practice.[24] It seems

[21] S.C.S. Off., 19 apr. 1899—*Fontes*, n. 1220; S.C.S. Off. (Cochinchin.), 1 aug. 1759—*Fontes*, n. 810; S. C. de Prop. Fide, 16 ian. 1797, ad 2—Coll. S.C.P.F., n. 634; *Fontes*, n. 4652.

[22] S. C. de Prop. Fide, instr., 16 ian. 1797, Coll. S.C.P.F., n. 634; *Fontes*, n. 4652.

[23] "De Clausula Restrictiva Cononi 1123 Adiecta,"—*ETL*, III (1926), 328-337.

[24] Vromant, *Ius Matrimoniale* (2. ed., 1938), n. 381; Payen, *De Matrimonio in Missionibus*, nn. 2262, 2279; Cappello, *De Matrimonio*, n. 770, Vlaming, *Praelectiones*, n. 721.

certain that, in view of the decree of the Holy Office and in the light of the principle of canon 1127, the convert does not jeopardize his right to a new marriage. The infidel is to be considered as having departed unjustly.

2. Culpable Moral Departure

It may happen also that the unconverted party agrees, indeed, to continue marital life with the convert but refuses to live peacefully without injury or insult to the Creator. This condition would be verified if the infidel had the intention of attempting to persuade the convert to renounce the faith enirely [25] or of leading the convert into participating in acts which would be seriously sinful.[26] If the infidel refuses to relinquish the practice of concubinage, or if he denies a christian education to the children of his marriage with the convert, these actions would constitute grave injury to he Creator. Despite his wish to continue marital relations, he really is guilty of unjust departure.[27]

A third situation which may be realized frequently, especially in mission territories, is that some physical impossibility may prevent the infidel from resuming peaceful cohabitation, even though this impossibility is not at all culpable on the part of the unbaptized party. A verification of this contingency is realized if the infidel is forcibly detained by creditors or by a second spouse.[28] The decree cited that out of justice the interpellations must be made at least once, and that out of charity they may be made several times.

The lapse of a just and reasonable time in which the infidel fails to return is required before the convert is free to contract a second union.[29] It is also necessary that, if it is possible for him to do so, the convert should remove the obstacle which prevents the unbeliever's

[25] S.C.S. Off. (Mongoliae), 29 nov. 1882, ad 3—*Fontes*, n. 1075.

[26] S. C. de Prop. Fide (ad C. P. pro Sin.—Tunkin. Occident.), 5 mart. 1816, ad 6—*Coll. S.C.P.F.*, n. 704; Fontes, n. 4697.

[27] S.C.S. Off. (Natal), 11 iul. 1866, ad 2-4—*Fontes*, n. 996; S.C.S. Off. (Tunkin Occident.), 14 dec. 1848, ad 2—*Fontes*, n. 908.

[28] S.C.S. Off. (Cochinchin. Occident.), 12 iun. 1850, ad 1—*Fontes*, n. 908.

[29] Payen, *De Matrimonio in Missionibus*, n. 2285.

return. Thus, if before the baptism of her spouse a woman had been sold even by some one other than her husband and, upon questioning, expressed her willingness to be converted or to live peacefully, the convert would be required to buy her back if he were able to do so. Should she fail to keep her promises, the convert would later be able to employ the Pauline Privilege.[30]

If the infidel has been taken away beyond all hope of recovery, or if she has been sold, even by her own consort, but before his conversion, then departure is considered to have taken place on the part of the infidel party.[31] It is evident that after the time of his baptism the convert must be innocent of causing the obstacle which prevents resumption of the marital relationship. The Congregation for the Propagation of the Faith has admitted perpetual insanity of an infidel spouse as a sufficient reason for a dispensation from the interpellations in order that the convert may contract a new marriage.[32]

It must be noted that the Holy See, in the many responses already cited, treats almost exclusively of the refusal of peaceful cohabitation on the part of the infidel from the viewpoint of the danger from a continuation of married life, of perversion for the convert or of grave insults to God. It is impossible to cite responses of the Roman Congregations to clarify the notion of physical departure which, on the part of the infidel, is blameless. Apart from the response of the Congregation for the Propagation of the Faith cited above, the Congregations have not, up to the present, settled the question of whether serious disease may constitute such a departure. Nor may much guidance from canonists be expected on this important question. Very few of them consider it.

But, certainly, whether attention be centered on problems that arise in this country or in mission countries, the question whether serious contagious and practically incurable disease constitutes an actual physical separation on the part of the infidel, even though he express the wish to be converted and to continue in peaceful cohabi-

30 S.C.S. Off. (Siam), 4 iul. 1855—*Fontes*, n. 931.

31 S.C.S. Off. (Victoriae Nyanzae), 8 iul. 1891, ad 1, 2—*Fontes*, 1140.

32 S. C. de Prop. Fide (ad C. P. pro Sin.—Sutchuen.) 5 mart. 1787, ad 1 —*Coll. S.C.P.F.*, n. 589; *Fontes*, n. 4615.

tation, is one of the greatest practical importance.[33] It is difficult to conceive of a marital union which would be more truly a servitude for the convert than one in which the unconverted party is suffering from a disease which, such as leprosy, or syphilis, or other venereal diseases, could be cured only after a period of intensive treatment. True married life would be impossible without the most certain danger of infection. Even though it must be granted that great advances have been made in medical skill, results are still uncertain and the dangers of infection still remain great.

Gasparri contends that such diseases do not constitute a just cause to admit the use of the Pauline Privilege.[34] But his reasoning is difficult to follow. He maintains that if the convert is suffering from leprosy, for example, the infidel is fully justified in refusing cohabitation. On the contrary, if the infidel is infected with leprosy, but in response to the interpellation indicates his wish to continue cohabitation, the convert can not use the Pauline Privilege inasmuch as the departure of the infidel is in no way realized. Such a use of the privilege, Gasparri contends, would be a cause of scandal and a violation of charity. Gasparri does not advert to the possibility that the departure of the infidel may be blameless but none the less real in such a case. His opinion does not seem to favor the convert or the faith; he is far more lenient in his attitude toward the infidel.[35]

Vromant [36] and Cappello [37] have no hesitation in admitting the availability of the privilege under these circumstances. They extend it, also, to those cases in which the crimes of the infidel are so notorious that cohabitation with him would be for the convert a source of infamy.[38] Vromant [39] indicates that the convert may have a grave obligation in charity to support an unconverted spouse who is seriously ill, but he does not question the right of the convert to use the Pauline Privilege.

[33] Payen, *De Matrimonio in Missionibus*, n. 2268 bis.
[34] *De Matrimonio*, n. 1152.
[35] Payen, *De Matrimonio in Missionibus*, nn. 2262 bis; 2286 bis.
[36] *Ius Matrimoniale* (1. ed. 1931), n. 310.
[37] *De Matrimonio*, n. 771.
[38] Cf. Vermeersch, *De Casu Apostoli*, n. 45.
[39] *Loc. cit.*, n. 310.

That such diseases and the emergence of grave infamy for the convert from the infidel's manner of life constitute a true departure is solidly probable. Otherwise it could be that many converts might be subject to a marital union which would be the most odious and intolerable servitude. The convert's choice would be between what for him would be two evils. He would have to live a celibate life for years, or perhaps for his lifetime, with the consequent danger of grave sin; or he would have to risk the danger of infection. The solution of such problems seems to be among the reasons that the principle of canon 1127 was enunciated in the Code.

There seems to be no solid argument to prevent a local ordinary from permitting the use of the Pauline Privilege under such circumstances. The alleged scandal arising from the new marriage of the convert with a Catholic may be effectively removed. The principle of canon 1127 would make such a solution of this vexing problem not only practical but safe and prudent.[40]

However, since this opinion is not incontrovertibly certain, the local ordinary, if he should judge that it involves too great an extension of canon 1127, may follow what is an unquestionably certain course by submitting each case to the Holy Office for its final decision. The Holy See, by granting a dispensation from all interpellations, may dissolve the marriage which was contracted and consummated in infidelity. But if due care is exercised in the investigation of each case, the same effect could be more conveniently and just as safely obtained by the use of canon 1127.

In concluding this treatment of the notion of departure on the part of the unconverted spouse, one must point out that in those cases in which the infidel is willing to cohabit peacefully and to abide by all the requirements of the law, even though he be unwilling to be converted, the convert may not use the Pauline Privilege to contract a new marriage. It cannot be set down as an unvarying rule that cohabitation with an infidel always carries with it the proximate danger of perversion for the convert. That would be to

[40] Payen, *De Matrimonio in Missionibus*, n. 2286 bis; Vromant, *Ius Matrimoniale* (1. ed., 1931) n. 310.

maintain that St. Paul erred in advising converts not to depart from an unconverted spouse.[41]

In a particular case, according to circumstances of place and person, there may be indications of this danger to faith.[42] It is the bishop's (ordinary's) grave duty to determine whether cohabitation is then to be permitted. Cappello[43] indicates that, theoretically, canon 1127 would permit the solution of a doubtful case in the convert's favor, but he qualifies the statement by recommending that, in practice, each case be submitted to the Holy See. This opinion requiring recourse to the Holy Office is by far the more common and the safer solution.[44]

B. *The Interpellations*

The departure of the unconverted spouse, whether that departure be physical or moral, is not to be presumed; it must be demonstrated. The normal way in which this departure will be demonstrated is through the formal declaration of the infidel in answer to the interpellations, first as to whether he desires to be converted and to receive baptism, and secondly as to whether at least he will cohabit with the convert peacefully and without insult to the Creator.[45]

Whether the interpellations are necessary by divine or by ecclesiastical law cannot be ascertained from any uniform view of the canonists, for no such uniformity of opinion exists. In general, authors arrive at their conclusions concerning the necessity of making the interpellations according to their teaching in relation to the immediate divine or the apostolic origin of the Pauline Privilege. The Holy Office in one response spoke of the necessity of the interpellations *ex divino praecepto*; but this reply cannot be construed as a specific anwser to the question regarding the origin of the law

[41] I Cor., VII: 12-13.

[42] S.C.S. Off., litt. 7 aug. 1891—*Fontes*, n. 1142; De Smet, *De Sponsalibus et Matrimonio*, n. 348.

[43] *De Matrimonio*, n. 773.

[44] De Becker, *De Sponsalibus et Matrimonio*, n. 447; De Smet, *De Sponsalibus et Matrimonio*, n. 348.

[45] Canon 1121.

which requires the interpellations. Nor was it a dogmatic definition; it was merely a disciplinary response.[46]

The Congregation for the Propagation of the Faith was asked directly if the interpellations were necessary by divine law, but in its reply the Congregation gave a practical solution of the difficulty presented and avoided the question on the origin of the law.[47] The dispute is not settled even now by the Code. But it is safe to defend the view that the necessity of making the interpellations is founded purely on ecclesiastical law,[48] and that as author of the law which requires the dispensations the Church is capable of dispensing and does dispense from both or from one of the questions, as she sees fit.[49]

The question of the divine or ecclesiastical origin of the requirement of the interpellations is a question apart from the one which deals with the necessity of the interpellations for the validity of the ensuing marriage. All authorities are agreed that for the licit use of the privilege the interpellations must be made. This requirement for the licit use of the privilege binds both by divine and ecclesiastical law. The only exception to this rule obtains in those cases which come under canon 1125 and those in which the Holy See or its delegates has dispensed. It is evident that the Holy See does not consider the uselessness or the impossibility or the dangers attendant upon the execution of the interpellations as implying, *ipso facto*, a dispensation from the necessity of making them.[50]

But there is no unanimity of opinion on the point whether the interpellations are required for the validity of the second marriage, or on the point which concerns the source of this obligation in the combined force of the divine and ecclesiastical law, or in the binding

46 S.C.S. Off. (Cochinchin. Occident.), 12 iun. 1850, ad 1—*Fontes*, n. 910; S.C.S. Off., instr. (ad Archiep. Quebecen.), 16 sept. 1824, ad 3—*Fontes*, n. 866.

47 S.C. de Prop. Fide—(cf. same document on p. 170. Tunk. Occident.), 5 mart. 1816, ad 1—*Coll. S.C.P.F.*, n. 704; *Fontes*, n. 4697.

48 Cappello, *De Matrimonio*, n. 778; Chelodi, *Ius Matrimoniale*, n. 158.

49 Canons 1121, § 2; 1123. Cf. De Smet, *De Sponsilibus et Matrimonibus*, n. 353; Wernz-Vidal, *Ius Matrimoniale*, n. 632; Cerato, *Matrimonium*, n. 121.

50 S.C.S. Off., instr. (ad Archiep. Quebecen.), 16 sept. 1824, ad 3—*Fontes*, n. 866; S.C.S. Off. (Portland), 18 iun. 1884—*Fontes*, n. 1088.

power of the ecclesiastical law alone. It is certainly safe to say that, if one judge from the principles established by the Holy Office and from the solutions given by it in particular cases,[51] the opinion of those pre-Code authors who held that if not by divine law, then at least by ecclesiastical law, the interpellations were necessary for the validity of the second marriage was solidly probable.[52]

Since the promulgation of the Code, even though the controversy may not be considered as definitively settled,[53] the law indicates the necessity of the interpellations *ad validitatem*. The text of canon 1121, § 1, reads: "Antequam coniunx conversus . . . *valide* contrahat, debet partem non baptizatum interpellare," and paragraph two of the same canon: "Hae interpellations fieri semper debent." Canon 1122, § 2, seems to favor the necessity of the interpellations also: "Interpellationes etiam privatim factae ab ipsa parte conversa *valent*." These canons appear to indicate that the interpellations are, by ecclesiastical law, always necessary for the validity of the subsequent marriage.[54]

Practically the law of the Code is clear. Either the interpellations must be made or a dispensation from them must be obtained. If, after a second marriage has been contracted, it is shown with *certainty* that the interpellations were not made, the nature of the case will determine the course to be pursued; at any rate, canon 1127 would not apply here.[55] But if an insoluble doubt arises as to whether the interpellations were made at all or proposed properly, it seems that canon 1127 may safely be employed to render the second marriage certainly valid. It is presumed, of course, that if the interpellations can be supplied safely this should be done. If they were supplied,

[51] S. C. de Prop. Fide. (Tunk. Occident.), 5 mart. 1816—*Coll. S.C.P.F.*, n. 704, ad 1; S.C.S. Off., (Pondicher), 20 iun. 1858—*Fontes*, n. 947; S.C.S. Off., (Correae), 11 sept. 1878—*Fontes*, n. 1057.

[52] Payen, *De Matrimonio in Missionibus*, n. 2354.

[53] Payen, *op. cit.*, n. 2255.

[54] Cappello, *De Matrimonio*, n. 776; Wernz-Vidal, *Ius Matrimoniale*, n. 632; De Smet, *De Sponsalibus et Matrimonio*, n. 349; Chelodi, *Ius Matrimoniale*, n. 158; Cerato, *Matrimonium*, n. 121.

[55] Payen, *De Matrimonio in Missionibus*, n. 2358; Vromant, *Ius Matrimoniale* (1. ed., 1931), n. 332; Gregory, *The Pauline Privilege*, p. 70.

or if a dispensation were obtained, the safer course in practice would be to have the parties renew their consent in order to assure the validity of the marriage, since, in that case, canon 1127 would play no part. But if it is practically impossible to obtain this renewal of consent, the parties should be left in good faith, according to the principle of canon 1127.[56]

1. THE RESPONSE OF THE INFIDEL

The questions to be asked of the unconverted party have been the same for centuries[57] and remain unchanged by the Code.[58] Two questions are to be asked of the infidel: 1. if he wishes to be converted and baptized; 2. if he wishes at least to live with the convert peacefully without blaspheming God. It is neither licit nor valid to ask only one or the other of the questions; both must be asked unless a declaration of the Holy See dispenses from this obligation.[59]

From the nature of the questions asked, several possibilities may be realized in the infidel's reply. First, he may answer both questions in the affirmative or both in the negative. Secondly, he may answer one in the affirmative and one in the negative. Third, he may refuse to give any response at all.

If the unconverted party answers both questions negatively, the convert acquires the right to enter a new marriage.[60] If he answers both questions affirmatively, that is, if he expresses his willingness to be baptized and to continue marital life, then the bond contracted

[56] Vromant, *Ius Matrimoniale* (1. ed., 1931), n. 332; Payen, *De Matrimonio in Missionibus*, n. 2359.

[57] Innocent III, ep. *Quanto te Magis*, 1 maii 1199—c. 7, X, *de divortiis*, IV, 19; ep. *Gaudemus in Domino*, 1201—c. 8, X, *de divortiis*, IV, 19; S.C.C., 23 ian. 1603—Benedictus XIV, *De Synodo Dioecesana*, lib. XIII, cap. XXI, n. 1; S.C.S. Off. (Cochinchin.), 1 aug. 1759—*Fontes*, n. 810; S.C.S. Off. (Victoriae Nyanzae), 8 iul. 1891—*Fontes*, n. 1140.

[58] Canon 1121, § 1.

[59] Canon 1121, § 2; S.C.S. Off., 10 dec. 1885—*Fontes*, n. 1097; Wernz-Vidal, *Ius Matrimoniale*, n. 632; Vermeersch, *De Casu Apostoli*, n. 54; Vermeersch-Creusen, *Epitome*, II, n. 431.

[60] Canon 1123; S.C.S. Off. (ad Vic. Ap. Yunnan), 23 iun. 1847—*Fontes*, n. 903; S.C.S. Off. (Siam), 17 iul. 1850—*Fontes*, n. 911.

in infidelity endures, since under these circumstances there is no departure and the convert acquires no right to a new marriage. However, if the infidel is detained for whatever reason from fulfilling his promises within the time set by the ordinary,[61] the convert may contract a new marriage.

In the second hypothesis, the unconverted party may answer the question as to his wish to be converted in the negative, but may express his willingness to live with the convert in peace and without injury to the Christian religion. If such an answer is given the convert acquires no right to a new marriage during the lifetime of her spouse, unless in the judgment of the ordinary the response of the infidel is to be considered as negative because of the grave spiritual danger threatening the soul of the convert from continued cohabitation.[62] An ordinary who possesses faculties permitting him to do so could dispense from the obligation of asking the infidel about his willingness to cohabit, if he were certain of the existence of this danger at the time when the interpellations are to be made.[63]

Should the infidel agree to be baptized but refuse peaceful cohabitation, even though after baptism the convert had given no just cause for departure, he is to be considered insincere in his response and the convert acquires the right to contract another marriage.[64]

Finally, if the infidel, although no legitimate obstacle prevents him, pays no attention to the interpellations and refuses to make any response, his action is to be construed as a negative reply and the convert is free to remarry.[65]

[61] S.C.S. Off. (Cochinchin. Occident.), 12 iun. 1850—*Fontes*, n. 910; (Siam), 22 nov. 1871—*Fontes*, n. 1019; (Victoriae Nyanzae), 8 iul. 1891—*Fontes*, n. 1140.

[62] S.C.S. Off. (Mongoliae), 29 nov. 1882—*Fontes*, n. 1075.

[63] S.C.S. Off. (Mongoliae), 29 nov. 1882—*Fontes*, n. 1075.

[64] S.C.S. Off. (Victoriae Nyanzae), 8 iul. 1891—*Fontes*, n. 1040; S.C.S. Off., 26 apr. 1899—*Fontes*, n. 1222; De Smet, *De Sponsalibus et Matrimonio;* Vermeersch, *De Casu Apostoli*, n. 60.

[65] Canon 1123; cf. Wernz-Vidal, *Ius Matrimoniale*, n. 632; Payen, *De Matrimonio in Missionibus*, n. 2368; Vromant, *Ius Matrimoniale*, n. 341; Vermeersch, *De Casu Apostoli*, n. 60.

2. THE VALUE OF THE RESPONSES

From the insistence which the Church places on the obligation of making the interpellations it is evident that the answers of the infidel are presupposed to be sincerely given. But if it is known for a certainty that these answers are insincere and that they were made out of ill will toward the convert, the affirmative replies of the infidel are to be considered as negative.[66] This case would be verified if the replies of the infidel were deliberately ambiguous and remained so though an opportunity was given him to clarify his response.[67] It would be verified also if the infidel refused to reply at all or if the response were continually and obstinately delayed for a period of six months,[68] or if the infidel remained in hiding lest he be reached.[69] A consideration of the nature of these possibilities affords sufficient grounds to justify the conclusion that the departure of the infidel is truly verified.

It must be noted, however, that the response of the Holy Office upon which this interpretation of the insincerity of the infidel's reply is based required that this insincerity be demonstrated by certain proof.[70] The Vicar Apostolic of Mongolia asked: What is to be thought of the affirmative reply of an infidel, namely, that he is willing to live peaceably, without contumely to the Creator, if there is solid ground for the fear that he may sell or give his converted wife to others? The Congregation replied that if the interpellation had not been made, the Vicar Apostolic should use his faculties to dispense in extraordinary cases. But if the interpellation had already been made and the evil disposition of the husband was proved by certain arguments, the Congregation directed that the affirmative reply be considered negative and that correspondingly

[66] S.C.S. Off. (Mongoliae), 29 nov. 1882—*Fontes*, n. 1075; S.C.S. Off., 28 nov. 1894—*ASS*, XXIX (1894), 564; Vermeersch, *De Casu Apostoli*, n. 60; Chelodi, *Ius Matrimoniale*, n. 158; Cappello, *De Matrimonio*, n. 780; Wernz-Vidal, *Ius Matrimoniale*, n. 632.

[67] Payen, *De Matrimonio in Missionibus*, n. 2368.

[68] S.C.S. Off. (Mongoliae), 29 nov. 1882—*Fontes*, n. 1075.

[69] Wernz-Vidal, *op. cit.*, n. 632; Payen, *op. cit.*, n. 2368.

[70] S.C.S. Off. (Mongoliae), 29 nov. 1882—*Fontes*, n. 1075.

the woman might marry again. But if certain proof was lacking, the Congregation demanded that each case be forwarded to the Holy See for solution. In other words, the Holy See reserved to itself the solution of doubts concerning the sincerity of the response to the interpellations.

In relation to canon 1127 it is of practical importance to determine whether this recourse to the Holy See must still be made should such doubts arise. Practically every canonist who has given more than cursory consideration to the principle of canon 1127 maintains that the solution of a probable doubt concerning the sincerity of the infidel's response to the interpellations falls within the limits of the canon.[71]

In view of he unanimity with which canonists admit the use of canon 1127 to settle such a doubt practically, safely and authoritatively, there should be no hesitation on the part of a local ordinary or his delegate to apply the principle of the canon under such circumstances. Canon 1127 should never be applied without due investigation which is calculated to dispel the doubt if that be possible. But if a probable doubt about the sincerity of such responses remains, the canon certainly is applicable.

The principle of canon 1127 is embodied in the general law of the Church and is, therefore, superior to a particular response of a Congregation. A second marriage contracted by a convert on the strength of the application of canon 1127 by the local ordinary would certainly be valid and licit. Payen, however, is of the opinion that unless the infidel gives expressly a negative answer, it is safer to ask a dispensation from the interpellations.[72] But it must be noted that, when he is treating expressly of canon 1127,[73] he admits the use of the canon without restriction. It is, therefore, not easy to see why

[71] Vromant, *Ius Matrimoniale*, (1. ed., 1931), n. 341; Cappello, *De Matrimonio*, nn. 780, 788; Léry, *Le Privilège de la Foi*, n. 114; Gasparri, *De Matrimonio*, n. 1168; Arendt, "Nota circa canonem 1127,"—*ETL*, I (1924), 183; Vermeersch-Creusen, *Epitome*, n. 437; De Smet, *De Sponsalibus Matrimonio*, n. 355; Pyaen, *De Matrimonio in Missionibus*, nn. 2368, 2415 bis; et alli omnes.

[72] *De Matrimonio in Missionibus*, n. 2368.

[73] *Op. cit.* n. 2415 bis.

t is safer to ask a dispensation *ad cautelam,* if canon 1127 may be applied at all. The canon would have exactly the same effect as the dispensation. If due care and prudence are exercised in its use, the principle of canon 1127 is as safe and as certain in effect as the dispensation.

3. DOUBT REGARDING THE SUFFICIENCY OF THE CAUSE FOR A DISPENSATION

It has been emphasized repeatedly that the interpellations must be made in every case, even when there is sufficient evidence that the infidel has no intention of being baptized or that he has already entered another marriage. But for a just cause the Holy Father may in an individual case dispense from the necessity of making the interpellations.[74] Such a dispensation may relax the need of proposing both question or only one of the questions; it may be given by the Holy See directly or through its delegate indirectly; it may be granted either by means of special faculties and indults[75] or in virtue of the law of the Code.[76]

For the purpose at hand it is not necessary to enter into a full discussion of the factor of dispensation from the making of the interpellations.[77] The question to be determined here is whether canon 1127 may be applied if there is a well-founded doubt as to the sufficiency of the cause for dispensing from the making of the interpellations.

a. Just Causes for Dispensation

A dispensation from the making of the interpellations in a particular case cannot be conceded unless there is present a just and

[74] Canons 1121, § 2; 1123.

[75] Formulae Facultatum Quas S. C. de Prop. Fide Ordinariis in Terris Missionum Procurat—cf. Veermersch-Creusen, *Epitome,* n. 873; *Formula III (Maior),* nn. 25, 26, 27; *Formula III (Minor),* nn. 24, 25, 26.

[76] Canon 1125.

[77] For full treatments confer: Gregory, *The Pauline Privilege,* nn. 76-90; Cappello, *De Matrimonio,* nn. 781-788; Payen, *De Matrimonio in Missionibus,* nn. 2395-2403; Vromant, *Ius Matrimoniale,* (1. ed., 1931), nn. 354-373.

reasonable cause, the existence of which has been determined at least by a summary extra-judicial investigation. In general terms, the Holy See has admitted as just causes for a dispensation the impossibility or inutility of making the interpellations and the grave danger which might arise for the convert if he should attempt to make the interpellations.[78] But more particularly these causes are divided into two classes, ordinary and extraordinary.

Among the ordinary causes are the following: a. the lack of knowledge as to the place of the infidel's present residence; b. a state of war or danger from brigands which makes safe access to the infidel's place of residence impossible; [79] c. the excessive distance that one would have to travel to make the interpellations; d. the failure of the infidel to reply within the appointed time; [80] e. the inability of a polygamist convert to remember who his first and legitimate wife was and his uncertainty as to the nature of the consent exchanged;[81] f. the difficulty of finding the first wife either because her identity is uncertain or because of the difficulty of locating her present place of residence.[82]

Extraordinary causes for dispensation contemplate those circumstances in which the infidel may be readily reached but there is present a manifest danger of serious harm to the convert or to other christians if the interpellations are made.[83] This danger may be realized even though the response of the infidel might be affirmative; but the danger should not be founded on mere presumptions.

b. Canon 1127 and Doubtful Causes

With these recognized causes for dispensation as a norm it will generally be possible for the ordinary who possesses the faculty of

[78] S.C.S. Off. (ad Vic. Ap. Iaponiae Merid.), 4 febr. 1891—*Fontes*, n. 1130; S.C.S. Off. 16 aug. 1895—ASS, XXIX (1895), 565.

[79] S.C.S. Off. (Mongoliae), 29 nov. 1882—*Fontes*, n. 1075.

[80] *Fontes*, n. 1075.

[81] Paulus III, *Altitudo*, Docum. VI, C.I.C.; S.C.S. Off. (Siouxormen.) 18 maii 1892—*Fontes*, n. 1155.

[82] Pius V, *Romani Pontificis*, 2 aug. 1571—Docum. VII, *C.I.C.;* S.C.S. Off. (Siam), 22 nov. 1871—*Fontes*, n. 1019.

[83] S.C.S. Off. (Chensi et Chansi), 23 nov. 1769—*Fontes*, n. 825; Facultates S. C. de Prop. Fide, *Formula III* (*Maior*), n. 26; (*Minor*), n. 25.

dispensing to determine with moral certainty the sufficiency of the cause alleged in a particular case for the obtaining of a dispensation. If differences of time and place and person are taken into consideration, it will be readily evident that it is almost impossible to cite a case to illustrate a doubtful cause.

But should such a doubt as to the impossibility or inutility or the danger of making the interpellations persist after careful investigation, canonists are unanimous in the opinion that, in virtue of canon 1127 and of canon 84, § 2, the dispensation may be lawfully requested and validly granted. In favor of the faith, the person having the faculty to dispense may judge in favor of the convert, for canon 1127 implies the intervention of the supreme ministerial power of the Pope, should it be necessary to dissolve the bond of a marriage contracted in infidelity.[84]

Article II. Canon 1127 and the Constitutions of Canon 1125

A. *The Constitution* ALTITUDO *of Paul III*

One of the concessions originally destined to affect only particular regions, but now extended to include individual cases in which the same circumstances required for their use are verified in these particular cases, wherever they may occur, is that of Paul III contained in the Constitution *Altitudo*.[85] Briefly, the favor granted by this

[84] Arendt, "Nota circa canonem 1127,"—*ETL*, I (1924), 184; Cappello, *De Matrimonio*, n. 788; Vermeersch-Creusen, *Epitome*, n. 437; Cerato, *Matrimonium*, n. 127; Gasparri, *De Matrimonio*, n. 1168; Léry, *Le Privilège de la Foi*, n. 114; Payen, *De Matrimonio in Missionibus*, n. 2415 bis; Vromant, *Ius Matrimoniale* (2. ed., 1938) n. 380; et alii omnes.

[85] Canon 1125; Docum. VI, C.I.C. If it may be said that it is seriously doubtful that the constitutions are intended not for cases but for countries or regions in a country, the principle of canon 1127 would nevertheless permit their use in a convert's favor in a *case* of similar import. But the arguments against the *local* interpretation are so strong that there seems to be little room for prudent doubt as to the nature of the extensive force of the canon. Cf. Burton, *A Commentary on Canon 1125* pp. 113-116; Woods, *The Constitutions of Canon 1125*, pp. 73-82; Léry, *Le Privilège de la Foi*, nn. 74-77.

constitution is the following: if a polygamous convert cannot remember whom of his several wives he married first, he may take from among them the one whom he wishes and contract marriage with her by exchanging matrimonial consent.[86] If the convert can recall who his first wife was, then no concession is made.[87] This first legitimate wife must be retained unless the Pauline Privilege may be applied.

Before this constitution can become applicable, the convert must have had at least two wives.[88] It must be noted also that, while the constitution speaks only of a man who cannot recall who was his first wife, the favor conceded applies also if a woman who has had several husbands cannot recall whom she had married legitimately.[89] In relation to canon 1127, practically all canonists list as one of the doubtful matters, which may be settled by the application of the principle of the canon, a doubt as to the person of the first wife of a polygamist convert.[90]

If the convert cannot recall who his first wife was, or if the identity of the first wife or the validity of the first marriage is doubtful, then canon 1127 can be employed to effect the certain dissolution of this doubtful bond. The constitution adds nothing to what could be obtained by the use of canon 1127, if a polygamist convert who cannot remember who his first wife was wishes to marry one of the other women with whom he has lived if she is not related to him within the second degree of consanguinity in the collateral

[86] Cf. Docum. VI, *C.I.C.*; Burton, *op. cit.*, pp. 138-142.

[87] The term "first wife" refers naturally to the woman with whom the convert contracted a valid marriage. If this legitimate wife has died and the convert later married validly again, the second wife would have to be retained. Cf. Payen, *De Matrimonio in Missionibus*, n. 2405, 1.

[88] Reg. 40, R. J. in VI°: *Pluralis locutio duorum numero est contenta.*

[89] S.C.S. Off., resp. (Cochin. Occident.), 12 iun. 1850—*Fontes*, n. 910; Payen, *op. cit.*, n. 2405; Vromant, *Ius Matrimoniale* (2. ed., 1938), n. 341.

[90] Payen, *De Matrimonio in Missionibus*, nn. 2405, 2415 bis; Vromant, *Ius Matrimoniale*, (2. ed., 1938), n. 374; Cappello, *De Matrimonio*, n. 788; Gasparri, *De Matrimonio*, n. 1168; Arendt, "Nota circa canonem 1127,"—*ETL*, I (1924), 182; Vermeersch-Creusen, *Epitome*, n. 437; Cerato, *Matrimonium*, n. 127.

line.[91] For by virtue of this constitution the impediment of consanguinity in the collateral line is reduced to the second degree inclusive for the convert who is permitted to make a choice among his former partners.[92] This provision does not apply to all polygamists. If the case of a polygamist does not come under this constitution, then the dispensation which is required in the case must be obtained.[93] Thus, if a marriage contracted in infidelity is doubtful because the person of the first wife is doubtful, it may be dissolved by the use of canon 1127. But any impediments which obstruct the validity of the new marriage must be removed by means of a direct dispensation.[94]

Another great concession of the constitution is that the convert polygamist may choose one of his partners (if he cannot remember who the first was) and contract a valid and lawful marriage with her, although she remains in infidelity.[95] The constitution itself seems to include a dispensation from the impediment of disparity of worship, but, in view of the uncertainty of canonists on this question, practically a dispensation should be obtained upon definite assurance that there is no proximate danger of perversion for the convert or for the children of the marriage whose Catholic education must be guaranteed.[96]

Essentially, then, Paul III allowed the convert to choose any one of the women with whom he had lived if he did not know who his first wife was. Her conversion was not required nor were those wives whom he had at an earlier time dismissed excluded from his choice.[97] Furthermore, the choice was not limited to one of the un-

[91] Payen, *op. cit.*, n. 2405.

[92] Docum. VI, C.I.C.

[93] Payen, *De Matrimonio in Missionibus*, n. 2405; Vermeersch-Creusen, *Epitome*, II, n. 436; Vromant, *Ius Matrimoniale* (2. ed., 1938), n. 341.

[94] Vromant, *Ius Matrimoniale* (2. ed., 1938), n. 369.

[95] Vermeersch-Creusen, *Epitome*, II, n. 436; Vromant, *op. cit.*, n. 342; Payen, *op. cit.*, n. 2405.

[96] Burton, *A Commentary on Canon 1125*, pp. 148-149; Payen, *op. cit.*, n. 2405 bis; Vromant, *Ius Matrimoniale* (1. ed., 1931), n. 357; (2. ed., 1938), n. 343; Vermeersch-Creusen, *Epitome*, II, 436; De Smet, *De Sponsalibus et Matrimonio*, n. 353.

[97] S. C. de Prop. Fide resp. (C. P. pro Sin-Tunkin, Orient.), 14 ian. 1806, ad 1—*Fontes*, 4686.

certain wives who wished to become a convert or to one who might already have been baptized.[98]

If a polygamist had lived with many women, but probability restricted the doubt as to who the first wife was to a small number among them, then canon 1127 would permit him to choose any one of his former partners. The identity of the first wife would still be doubtful and there is no indication that the constitution required the convert's choice to be limited to the few concerning whom the doubt existed that one of them was his first wife.[99]

But there can be no doubt that a convert whose first marriage is doubtful as the result of a doubt about the identity of the first wife may, in virtue of canon 1127, choose any woman, not necessarily one of his former partners, provided only that the wife so chosen herself become baptized. For canon 1127 may be applied only in such a case wherein the convert intends to marry a Catholic. It is precisely in this manner that its application to the Constitution *Altitudo* is to be understood.[100]

B. *The Constitutions* ROMANI PONTIFICIS *and* POPULIS OF *St. Pius V and Gregory XIII*

In the course of this study the Constitutions of St. Pius V and Gregory XIII have already received considerable attention. Since the purpose of the present study is not a commentary on canon 1125, but a consideration of the application of the principle of canon 1127 to the constitutions which by canon 1125 are made universal laws, little can be added to what has already been said of their application.

In special reference to the Constitution *Romani Pontificis*[101] it may be noted that the concession comprises four elements which pre-

[98] Vromant, *op. cit.* (2. ed., 1938), n. 342.

[99] Burton, *A Commentary on Canon 1125*, p. 146.

[100] S.C.S. Off., 8 iun. 1836—*Fontes*, n. 874; S.C.S. Off., instr. (ad Vic. Ap. Oceaniae Central.), 18 dec. 1872—*Fontes*, n. 1024; S.C.S. Off., instr. (ad Ep. S. Alberti), 9 dec. 1874—*Fontes*, n. 1036; S.C.S. Off., instr. (ad Vic. Ap. Iaponiae Merid.) 4 febr. 1891—*Fontes*, n. 1130. Cf. Constitution *Romani Pontificis*, 2 aug. 1571—Docum. VII, C.I.C.

[101] Docum. VII, C.I.C.

suppose that: 1. the first marriage of the polygamist was contracted while both parties were unbaptized; 2. the first wife is certainly known, but has not yet been baptized, nor has she expressed a desire to be baptized; 3. the party with whom the convert wishes to contract a new marriage, and who is not the first wife, is willing to be baptized with the convert; 4. it would be too great a hardship to demand the separation of the convert from the partner who wishes to be baptized with him.

From what has been said in the course of the whole study, both the need that may arise for the application of canon 1127 as well as the solution of the difficulties involved should be clear. It may be noted, however, that canon 1127 may not be applied to allow the convert to contract a marriage with another, even though the first and legitimate wife is ready and willing to be baptized. The basis of canon 1127 is the favor of the faith; it is intended to be of aid in the salvation of souls. To disregard the rights of a legitimate wife in such cases would tend to promote hatred of the Catholic Religion on the part of the one whose rights are not being recognized, and thus in all probability would become a detriment rather than an aid to conversion. This certainly is foreign to the mind of the legislator.[102]

In reference to the Constitution *Populis*[103] it is evident that it leaves little room for the applicaion of canon 1127 except in the same matters that were treated in this connection under the Pauline Privilege. For the notion of the impossibility of making the interpellations, which must be established in at least a summary extrajudicial investigation according to Gregory XIII's constitution, is to be determined in the light of the discussion of the departure of the infidel and of just causes for a dispensation from the making of the interpellations.[104]

[102] Cf. Burton, A *Commentary on Canon 1125*, p. 159; Woods, *The Constitutions of Canon 1125*, pp. 54-55; Payen, *op. cit.*, n. 2407; Vromant, *op. cit.* (2. ed., 1938), n. 344; Léry, *Le Privilège de la Foi*, n. 83.

[103] Docum. VIII, C.I.C.

[104] Burton, A *Commentary on Canon 1125*, p. 168; cf. *supra*, Chapter IX, art. I.

The great advantage of this constitution is that it provides the local ordinary, pastors and quasi-pastors,[105] and confessors of the Society of Jesus with the faculty to dispense from the interpellations when, after a summary extrajudicial investigation, it is evident that it is at least morally impossible to make them, or that after the questions had been asked the response has not been made in due time. It may be noted that this concession is not limited in its application to polygamists. Here, as in the other constitutions mentioned as well as in the use of the Pauline Privilege, the marriage must have been contracted in infidelity. If one party was doubtfully baptized, the case must be sent to the Holy See; the local ordinary may not apply canon 1127 to solve such a case.

Article III. The Effect of the Application of Canon 1127

A. *The Limitations of the Canon*

Since the juridic basis of canon 1127 is the power which the Pope has, as Vicar of Christ, to dissolve the bond of marriage which is not a consummated sacramental union, if the good of the faith demands his intervention, it must be morally certain that the case under consideration comes within the limits of this power. The Holy Father would never risk attempting to dissolve a bond when its dissolution does not certainly fall within the sphere of his supreme ministerial power. Otherwise there would be grave danger of approving an invalid and adulterous union. Certainly this is entirely contrary to the practice of the Church [106] and to the norms established
1796; *Fontes*, n. 1155.
in the Code.[107]

When it is evident that canon 1127 may be safely applied to render certain the dissolution of a doubtful bond contracted in infidelity, or to safeguard the validity of a marriage to be contracted through the application of the Pauline Privilege, as long as all the requisite conditions are not certainly fulfilled, then the supreme

[105] Cf. Burton, *op. cit.*, pp. 172-174.

[106] S.C.S. Off. (Siouxormen.), 19 maii 1892,ad 2—*Coll. S.C.P.F.*, n. 1796; *Fontes*, n. 1155.

[107] Canons 1069, § 2; 1076, § 3.

power of the Pope does dissolve the bond which is an obstacle to the Christian marriage, insofar as this intervention is necessary. But it does not grant a dispensation from any impediment, whether certainly or doubtfully present, diriment impediment. These impediments have no direct relationship to the former marriage which is to be dissolved. They affect the second marriage and the proper dispensation must be obtained as in the case of any other marriage.[108]

One may not after any fashion consider the application of canon 1127 to be the equivalent of a radical sanation of the second marriage. The Holy Father does not and cannot supply the consent of the parties who wish to marry. Thus Paul III in his Constitution *Altitudo* demanded that matrimonial consent be exchanged "*per verba de praesenti.*" [109] This requirement is clearly set forth in several instructions of the Holy Office when there is question of rendering certain, in favor of the faith, the validity of a doubtful marriage.[110]

According to the instructions just cited, if it should be morally impossible to obtain this renewal of consent, then as long as only one party in the doubtful union is converted, the convert may be left in possession of the marriage. This solution is an application of the principle of canon 1014. In similar circumstances it may always be safely employed.[111]

B. *The Time of the Dissolution of the First Marriage*

From the twelfth or thirteenth century it has been held as certain that a union contracted in infidelity is dissolved only when the convert in using the Pauline Privilege has entered a second marriage. But there is no unanimity of opinion as to the verification of this principle when there is question of the wider privilege of the faith. There seems to be no difficulty in relation to the dissolution of the natural bond of marriage when a dispensation of the Holy See inter-

108 Vromant, *Ius Matrimoniale* (2. ed., 1938), n. 369.

109 Docum. VI, C.I.C.

110 S.C.S. Off., instr. (ad Vic. Ap. Oceaniae Central.), 18 dec. 1872, ad 1, 2, 5—*Fontes*, n. 1024; S.C.S. Off., instr. (ad Ep. S. Alberti), 9 dec. 1874 —*Fontes*, n. 1036.

111 Vromant, *Ius Matrimoniale* (2. ed., 1938), n. 370.

venes as in the Helena Case. It seems that in such circumstances the bond of the former marriage is dissolved directly to permit a new marriage.[112]

But authors are divided with reference to the question of the point of time at which the dissolution of the prior marriage takes place when the faculties mentioned in the constitutions of canon 1125 are employed to prepare the way for the contraction of the later Christian marriage.[113] Prat is of the opinion that, if the faculties mentioned in the constitutions of St. Pius V and of Gregory XIII are invoked, the bond of the former marriage is dissolved from the moment that they are applied. Benedict XIV[114] held that the dissolution even in these cases was effected by the second marriage. Gasparri[115] is of the opinion that the doctrinal statement of canon 1126 applies also to the dissolution of the natural bond through a Papal dispensation. But he indicates that the question is not authoritatively settled, and points out that if the validity of a marriage depends on the applicability of canon 1126 to the privilege of the faith, the case must be submitted to the Holy Office. Jelicic,[116] after examining the question thoroughly, adopts Gasparri's opinion. He maintains that the privilege of the faith confers, like the Pauline Privilege, only the right to contract a new marriage.

In relation to canon 1127 two possibilities may be realized. If the principle of the canon is employed to permit the use of the Pauline Privilege, the first marriage would be dissolved at the time of the second marriage. And, in Vromant's opinion, the certain dissolution of the doubtful bond would be effected by the second marriage

[112] Léry, *Le Privilège de la Foi*, n. 25.

[113] *The Theology of St. Paul*, translated from the XI French Edition by John L. Stoddard (2 vols., London: Burns, Oates and Washbourne, 1926), I, 115.

[114] *De Synodo Dioecesana*, lib. XIII, cap. XXI, n. 5.

[115] *De Matrimonis*, n. 1167.

[116] "De Privilegio Fidei Eiusque Fundamento Juridico,"—*Jus Pontificium*, XVII (1937), 156-159.

(always with the exception of the Helena Case) in cases in which canon 1127 might be invoked.[117]

[117] Vromant, *Ius Matrimoniale* (2. ed., 1938), n. 371. Cf. also S.C.S. Off., instr. (ad Vic. Ap. Oceaniae Central.), 18 dec. 1872—*Fontes*, n. 1024; S.C.S. Off., instr. (ad Ep. S. Alberti), 9 dec. 1874—*Fontes*, n. 1036.

CONCLUSIONS

1. There exists in ecclesiastical jurisprudence a general principle that in any doubtful matter judgment should be in favor of the faith.

2. This principle was first clearly enunciated by Benedict XIV whose legal phraseology was adapted in the wording of canon 1127, which represents the only application in the Code of this general principle.

3. The principle of canon 1127 depends intrinsically on the existence and the application of the supreme ministerial power of the Pope, as Vicar of Christ, to dissolve the bond of a legitimate marriage if the bond really exists.

4. The Constitutions *Altitudo* of Paul III and *Romani Pontificis* of St. Pius V reprensent the first historical application of the principle now embodied in canon 1127.

5. The Congregation of the Holy Office applies this principle frequently to settle doubts in regard to the use of the Pauline Privilege. The Congregation noted expressly that this procedure represented a particular application of the general principle enunciated by Benedict XIV.

6. (a) The application of canon 1127 is not limited to the Pauline Privilege in the strict sense of that term for the canon may also be applied to the constitutions of canon 1125. The wide interpretation to be given to the rule of canon 1127 extends the phrase "privilege of the faith" to its widest signification.

(b) The nature of the doubt which permits the use of canon 1127 does not demand grave probable reasons for each proposition. It suffices that it be a doubt which excludes moral certitude for one side or the other.

7. An insolubly doubtful marriage between unbaptized partners may be considered either as valid or as invalid—(1) to permit the convert to contract a new marriage with a Catholic; (2) to render certain the validity of the new convert's marriage already contracted with a Catholic; (3) to renew matrimonial consent and to continue cohabitation with an unbaptized partner; and (4) to continue in

possession in the case of a doubtful marriage which because of the ill-will of the unbaptized partner cannot by renewal of consent be rendered certain in its status.

8. Canon 1127 may be applied by a local ordinary in order to permit the use of the Pauline Privilege for the sake of dissolving the doubtful bond of a marriage when marriage was contracted without a dispensation from the impediment of disparity of worship between a person *doubtfully baptized in the Catholic Church* and a person who is certainly not baptized.

9. A well founded doubt about the sincerity of the infidel's response to the interpellations may, in virtue of canon 1127, be decided by the local ordinary in favor of the convert as also may doubt as to the sufficiency of the cause for granting a dispensation from the interpellations by one empowered to dispense.

10. Canon 1127 may be applied only in order to permit a marriage with a Catholic. The application of the privilege granted by this canon dissolves the former marriage, but in relation to the second marriage it does not bestow or produce a sanation for an extant invalid union, nor does it imply or carry with it the effect of a dispensation from existing matrimonial impediments prior to the celebration of that marriage.

BIBLIOGRAPHY

Sources

Acta Apostolicae Sedis, Commentarium Officiale, Romae, 1909—

Acta Sanctae Sedis, 41 vols., Romae, 1865-1908.

Annuario Pontificio per l'Anno 1939, Città del Vaticano: Tipographia Vaticana, 1939.

Bullarum Diplomatum et Privilegiorum Sanctorum Romanorum Pontificum Taurinensis Editio, 24 vols., appendix, Augustae Taurinorum-Neapoli, 1857-1872.

Codex Iuris Canonici Pii X Pontificis Maximi iussu digestus Benedicti Papae XV auctoritate promulgatus, Romae: Typis Polyglottis Vaticanis 1917.

Codicis Iuris Canonici Fontes cura Emi. Petri Card. Gasparri editi, 9 vols., Romae (later, Civitate Vaticana): Typis Polyglottis Vaticanis, 1923-1939, (vols. VII-IX ed cura et studio Emi. Iustiniani Card. Serédi.

Collectanea S. Congregationis de Propaganda Fide, Romae, 1893.

Collectanea S. Congregationis de Propaganda Fide, 2 vols., Romae, 1907.

Corpus Iuris Canonici, editio Lipsiensis secunda, denuo edidit Aemilius Ludovicus Richter et Aemilius Freidberg, 2 vols., Lipsiae, 1879-1881.

Decretales D. Gregorii Papae IX, una cum Glossa Restituta, Romae, 1582.

Denzinger, Henricus, et Bannwart, Clemens, *Enchiridion Symbolorum Definitionum et Declarationum de Rebus Fidei et Morum,* 16 et 17 ed., Friburgi-Brisgoviae: Herder, 1928.

Friedberg, Aemilius, *Quinque Compilationes Antiquae,* Lipsiae, 1882.

Mansi, Joannes, *Sacrorum Conciliorum Nova et Amplissima Collectio,* 53 vols., Parisiis-Arnhem-Lipsiae, 1901-1927.

Reference Works

Alford, Culver Bernard, *Ius Matrimoniale St. Foed. Americae cum Iure Canonico Comparatum,* Kenedy: New York, 1938.

Aquinas, Thomas, St., *Divi Thomae Aquinatis Opera,* 2. ed., Veneta, 28 vols., Venetiis, 1775-1788.

Augustine, C., *A Commentary on the New Code of Canon Law,* 4. ed., revised, 8 vols., St. Louis: Herder, 1918-1929.

Ballerini, Antonius,—Palmieri, Dominicus, *Opus Theologicum Morale,* 2. ed., 7 vols., Prati, 1888-1892.

Barbosa, Augustinus, *Collectanea Doctorum tam Veterum quam Recentiorum in Ius Pontificium Universum,* 5 vols. in 4, Lugdini, 1656.

Benedictus XIV, *De Synodo Dioecesana,* 2 vols., Romae, 1767.

————*Opera Omnia,* 17 vols. in 18, Prati, 1843-1847.

Billot, Ludovicus, *De Ecclesiae Sacramentis Commentarium in Tertiam Partem S. Thomae,* 6 ed., 2 vols., Romae, 1922.

Blat, Albertus, *Commentarium Textus Codicis Iuris Canonici,* 5 vols. in 6, Romae: Ferrari, 1921-1927.

Bouscaren, T. Lincoln, *Canon Law Digest,* 2 vols. and *Supplement*—1941, Milwaukee: Bruce, 1934-1941.

Burton, Francis James, *A Commentary on Canon 1125,* The Catholic University of America, Canon Law Studies, n. 121, Washington, D. C.: The Catholic University of America Press, 1940.

Cajetanus, Cardinalis, *Opuscula Omnia D. Thomae de Vio in Tres Distinctos Tomos,* cf. p. 88, Lugduni, 1585.

Cappello, Felix M., *Tractatus Canonico-Moralis de Sacramentis,* 3 vols. in 6. Vol. III, *De Matrimonio,* 4. ed., Taurinorum Augustae: Marietti, 1939.

————*De Curia Romana,* 2 vols., Romae, 1911.

Cerato, Prosdocimus, *Matrimonium a Codice I. C. Integre Desumptum,* 4. ed., Pativii: Typis Seminarii Patavini, 1929.

Chelodi, Joannes, *Ius Matrimoniale,* 4. ed., recognita et aucta a Vigilio Dalpiaz, Tridenti: A. Ardesi, 1937.

Cicogani, Amleto Giovanni, *Canon Law,* 2. rev. ed., Philadelphia: Dolphin Press, 1935.

Cornelius a Lapide, *Commentaria in Scripturam Sacram,* Parisiis, 1866.

————*Commentarium in Omnes Divi Pauli Epistolas,* 2. ed., Hieronymus Albritius, Venetiis, 1717.

Cornely, Rudolphus, *Commentarium in S. Pauli Apostoli Epistolas,* Tom II, *Prior Epistola ad Corinthios,* 2. ed., Parisiis, 1909.

De Becker, Iulius, *Praelectiones Canonicae de Matrimonio,* ed. nova ad tramites Codicis Iuris Canonici accommodata, Louvanii: Fr. Ceuterick, 1931.

De Smet, A., *Tractatus Theologico-Canonicus de Sponsalibus et Matrimonio,* 4. ed., Brugis: Beyaert, 1927.

Dale, Alfred, W., *The Synod of Elvira,* London, 1882.

Fahrner, Ignaz, *Geschichte des Unauflöslichkeits prinzips und der vollkommenen Scheidung der Ehe im kanonischen Recht,* Frieburg im Breisgau, 1903.

Farrugia, Nicolaus, *De Matrimonio et Causis Matrimonialibus, Tractatus Canonico-Moralis Iuxta Codicem Iuris Canonici,* Romae, 1924.

Feije, Henricus Joannes, *De Impedimentis et Dispensationibus Matrimonialibus*, 3. ed., Lovanii, 1885.

Gasparri, Petrus, *Tractatus Canonicus de Matrimonio*, ed. nova ad mentem Codicis I. C., 2 vols., Romae: Typis Polyglottis Vaticanis, 1932.

Gigot, Francis E., *Christ's Teaching Concerning Divorce*, New York, 1912.

Giovine, Petrus, *Consultationes Canonicae de Dispensationibus Matrimonialibus*, 2 vols., Neapoli, 1843-1866.

Gregory, Donald J., *The Pauline Privilege*, The Catholic University of America Canon Law Studies, n. 68, Washington, D. C.: The Catholic University of America, 1931.

Gury, Joannes Petrus—Ballerini, Antonius, *Compendium Theologiae Moralis*, 2. ed., Romae-Taurini, 1869.

Hefele, Carolus—LeClercq, Henricus, *Histoire des Conciles*, Nouvelle Traduction Française Faite sur La Deuxième Edition Allemande, 10 vols. in 19, Paris, 1907-1938.

Hostiensis (Henricus de Segusio), *Commentaria in Quinque Libros Decretalium*, 5 vols. in 3, Venetiis, 1581.

Joyce, George Hayward, *Christian Marriage*, London and New York, Sheed & Ward, 1933.

Knecht, Augustus, *Handbuch des katholischen Eherechts*, Herder: Freiburg im Breisgau, 1928.

Lehmkuhl, Augustinus, *Theologia Moralis*, 5. ed., 2 vols., Friburgi Brisgoviae, 1888.

Léry, Louis Chaussegros de, *Le Privilège de la Foi*, Montreal: Collection des Studia Collegii Maximi I. C., 1938.

Liguori, Alphonsus, St., *Theologia Moralis*, editio nova, cura et studio P. Loenardi Gaudé, C. SS. R., 4 vols., Romae, Typis Polyglottis Vaticanis, 1905-1912.

Lugo, Joannes de, *Opera Omnia*, 7 toms. in 4 vols., Venetiis, 1718.

Michiels, Gommarus, *Normae Generales Iuris Canonici*, 2 vols., Lublin, Polonia, Universitas Catholica, 1929.

Migne, Jacobus Paulus, *Patrologiae Cursus Completus, Series Graeca*, 161 vols., Parisiis, 1856-1866.

———*Patrologiae Cursus Completus, Series Latina*, 221 vols., Parisiis, 1844-1855.

Noldin, H.,—Schmitt, A., *Summa Theologiae Moralis iuxta Codicem Iuris Canonici*, Vol. I, 32. ed., De Principiis, Oeniponte-Lipsiae: Rauch, 1939.

Palmieri, Dominicus, *Tractatus de Matrimonio Christiano*, Romae, 1880.

Panormitanus (Nicholaus de Tudeschis), *Commentaria in Quinque Libros Decretalium*, 5 vols. in 7, Venetiis, 1588.

Payen, G., *De Matrimonio in Missionibus ac Potissimum in Sinis Tractatus Practicus et Casus,* 2. ed., 3 vols., Zi-ka-Wei: Typographia T'OU-SE-WE, 1935-1936.

Perrone, Joannes, *De Matrimonio Chirtsiano Libri Tres,* 3 vols., Romae, 1858.

————*Praelectiones Theologicae,* 32. ed., Taurini, 1868.

Pesch, Christianus, *Praelectiones Dogmaticae,* 3. ed., 9 vols., Friburgi Brisgoviae, 1909.

Pontius, Basilius, *De Sacramento Matrimonii Tractatus,* 2. ed., Bruxellis, 1627.

Reiffenstuel, Anacletus, *Ius Canonicum Universum,* 5 vols. in 7, Parisiis, 1864-1882.

Rosset, M., *De Sacramento Matrimonii,* 6 vols., Parisiis, 1895-1896.

Sanchez, Thomas, *De Sancto Matrimonii Sacramento Disputationum Libri Decem in Tres Tomos Distributi,* Venetiis, 1712.

Santi, Franciscus, *Praelectiones Iuris Canonici,* 2 vols., Ratisbonae, 1885-1886.

Schenk, Francis J., *The Matrimonial Impediments of Mixed Religion and Disparity of Cult,* The Catholic University of America Canon Law Studies, n. 51, Washington, D. C.: The Catholic University of America Press, 1929.

Schmalzgrueber, Franciscus, *Ius Ecclesiasticum Universum,* 5 vols. in 12, Romae, 1843-1845.

Schönsteiner, Ferdinand, *Grundriss des kirchlichen Eherechts,* 2. ed., revised, Wien: Ludwig Auer, 1937.

Suarez, Franciscus, *Opera Omnia,* ed. C. Berton, 28 vols., Parisiis, 1856-1878.

Techo, Nicolaus del, *Historia Provinciae Paraquariae Societatis Jesu,* Leodii, 1673.

Toso, A., *Ad Codicem Juris Canonici Commentaria Minora,* 5 vols., Vol. I, 2. ed., Romae, 1921.

Triebs, Franz, *Praktisches Handbuch des geltenden kanonischen Eherechts, in Vergleichung mit dem deutschen staatlichen Eherecht,* Breslau: Ostdeutsche Verlagsanstalt, 1933.

Van Hove, A., *Commentarium Lovaniense in Codicem Iuris Canonici,* Vol. I, Tom. II, *De Legibus Ecclesiasticis,* Mechliniae—Romae: Dessain, 1930.

Vermeersch, Arthurus, *De Matrimoniali Casu Quem Apostoli Vocant seu de Fidei Privilegio,* Brugis, 1911.

Vermeersch, Arthurus, et Creusen, Josephus, *Epitome Iuris Canonici,* 3 vols., *Vol. I,* 6. ed., *Vols. II-III,* 5. ed., Mechliniae-Romae: Dessain, 1934-1937.

Vlaming, Th. M., *Praelectiones Iuris Matrimonii ad Normam Codicis Iuris Canonici*, 3. ed., 2 vols., Bussum in Hollandia: Sumptibus Societatis Editricis Anonymae, 1919-1921.

Vromant, G., *Facultates Apostolicae Quas Sacra Congregatio de Propaganda Fidei Delegare Solet Ordinariis Missionum, Commentaria in Formulam Tertiam*, Lovanii: Museum Lessianum, 1926.

————*Ius Missionariorum*, Vol. V, *De Matrimonio*, Lovanii: Museum Lessianum, 1931.

————*Ius Missionariorum*, Vol. V, *De Matrimonio*, 2. ed., Bruxellis-Parisiis: Museum Lessianum, 1938.

Wahl, Francis X., *The Matrimonial Impediments of Consanguinity and Affinity*, The Catholic University of America Canon Law Studies, n. 90, Washington, D. C.: The Catholic University of America, 1934.

Wernz, Franciscus X., et Vidal, Petrus, *Ius Canonicum ad Codicis Normam Exactum*, 7 toms. in 8 vols., Romae: apud Aedes Universitatis Gregorianae, 1923-1938.

Woods, Francis F., *The Constitutions of Canon 1125 and Their Application in the United States*, Milwaukee: Bruce, 1935.

Ziegler, Aloysius K., *Church and State in Visigothic Spain*, The Catholic University of America, Washington, D. C., 1930.

Zitelli, Zephyrinus, *De Dispensationibus Matrimonialibus*, Romae, 1884.

Periodicals

Apollinaris, Romae, 1928—

Ecclesiastical Review, The (originally *The American Ecclesiastical Review*), Philadelphia, 1889—

Ephemerides Theologicae Lovanienses, Brugis, 1924—

Jus Pontificium, Romae, 1921—

La Civiltà Cattolica, Romae, 1849—

Nouvelle Revue Théologique, Paris, 1869—

Periodica de Re Canonica et Morali utili praesertim Religiosis et Missionariis, Brugis, 1905—; ab anno 1927: *Periodica de Re Morali, Canonica, Liturgica*.

Articles

Arendt, G., "Quomodo in favorem fidei solvatur a S. Pontifice matrimonium in infidelitate contractum, Nota theologico-canonica circa canonem 1127," —*Ephemerides Theologicae Lovanienses*, I (1924), 174-184.

Creusen, Josephus, "Baptême Douteux et Mariage Indissoluble,"—*Nouvelle Revue Théologique*, LII (1925), 227-241.

———"De dubio matrimonio ob dubium baptismum,"—*Periodica*, XVII (1938), 153*-159*

Dalpiaz, Vigilius, "Annotationes ad Decretum S. C. Sancti Officii, die 10a. iunii 1937," *Apollinaris*, X (1937), 333-339.

Hürth, F., "Annotationes ad Decretum S. C. Sancti Officii,"—*Periodica*, XXVI (1937), 473-475.

Jelicic, V., De Priviligio Fidei Ejusque Fundamento Juridico, Jus Pontificium. XVII (1937), 156-169.

Kelly, James P., "Recent Decree on Doubtful Baptism and the Pauline Privilege,"—*Ecclesiastical Review*, XCVII (1937), 366-372.

———"La Potesta del Papa intorno al Matrimonio degli Infedeli,"—*La Civiltà Cattolica*, series 13, XI (1888), 664-696.

O'Connor, William R., "The Indissolubility of a Ratified Consummated Marriage," *Ephemerides Theologicae Lovanienses*, XII (1936), 692-722.

Rayanna, Puthota, "De Constitutione S. Pii Papae V, *Romani Pontificis*, 2 augusti 1571,"—*Periodica*, XXVII (1938), 295-331; XXVII (1939), 24-52, 112-134, 190-209.

Vermeersch, Arthurus, "Interpretatio Canonis 1127, de favore iuris concesso privilegio Fidei,"—*Periodica*, X (1921), (25)-(28).

Vromant, G., "Le Privilège de la Foi au Canon 1127,"—*Nouvelle Revue* Théologique, LIX, (1932), 440.

———"De applicatione Canonis 1127,"—*Jus Pontificium*, XII (1932), 114.

Abbreviations

AAS—*Acta Apostolicae Sedis.*

ASS—*Acta Sanctae Sedis.*

AKKR—*Archiv für katholisches Kirchenrecht.*

Coll. S.C.P.F.—*Collectanea S. Congregationis de Propaganda Fide.*

ER—*Ecclesiastical Review.*

ETL—*Ephemerides Theologicae Lovanienses.*

MPG—Migne, *Patrologia Series Graeca.*

MPL—Migne, *Patrologia Series Latina.*

NRT—*Nouvelle Revue Theologique.*

ALPHABETICAL INDEX

BIOGRAPHICAL NOTE

Francis Patrick Kearney was born in Baltimore, Maryland on October 25, 1911. He attended the parochial school of St. John the Evangelist. He entered St. Charles' College, Catonsville, Maryland, in 1926, and was graduated in 1931. In September, 1931, he entered St. Mary's Seminary and University, where he received the degree of Bachelor of Arts in 1933, of Bachelor of Sacred Theology in 1935, and of Lector of Sacred Theology in 1937. After two years in parish work at St. Joseph's Parish and the Basilica of the Assumption, Baltimore, he was enrolled in the School of Canon Law at the Catholic University of America in September, 1939, and received the Baccalaureate of Canon Law in June, 1940. He received the Licentiate in June, 1941.

CANON LAW STUDIES

1. Freriks, Rev. Celestine A., C.PP.S., J.C.D., Religious Congregations in Their External Relations, 121 pp., 1916.
2. Galliher, Rev. Daniel M., O.P., J.C.D., Canonical Elections, 117 pp., 1917.
3. Borkowski, Rev. Aurelius L., O.F.M., J.C.D., De Confraternitatibus Ecclesiasticis, 136 pp., 1918.
4. Castillo, Rev. Cayo, J.C.D., Disertacion Historico-Canonica sobre la Potestad del Cabildo en Sede Vacante o Impedida del Vicario Capitular, 99 pp., 1919 (1918).
5. Kubelbeck, Rev. William J., S.T.B., J.C.D., The Sacred Pentitentiaria and Its Relations to Faculties of Ordinaries and Priests, 129 pp., 1918.
6. Petrovits, Rev. Joseph J.C., S.T.D., J.C.D., The New Church Law On Matrimony, X-461 pp., 1919.
7. Hickey, Rev. John J., S.T.B., J.C.D., Irregularities and Simple Impediments in the New Code of Canon Law, 100 pp., 1920.
8. Klekotka, Rev. Peter J., S.T.B., J.C.D., Diocesan Consultors, 179 pp., 1920.
9. Wanenmacher, Rev. Francis, J.C.D., The Evidence in Ecclesiastical Procedure Affecting the Marriage Bond, 1920 (Printed 1935).
10. Golden, Rev. Henry Francis, J.C.D., Parochial Benefices in the New Code, IV-119 pp., 1921 (Printed 1925).
11. Koudelka, Rev. Charles J., J.C.D., Pastors, Their Rights and Duties According to the New Code of Canon Law, 211 pp., 1921.
12. Melo, Rev. Antonius, O.F.M., J.C.D., De Exemptione Regularium, X-188 pp., 1921.
13. Schaaf, Rev. Valentine Theodore, O.F.M., S.T.B., J.C.D., The Cloister, X-180 pp., 1921.
14. Burke, Rev. Thomas Joseph, S.T.D., J.C.D., Competence in Ecclesiastical Tribunals, IV-117 pp., 1922.
15. Leech, Rev. George Leo, J.C.D., A Comparative Study of the Constitution, "Apostolicae Sedis" and the "Codex Juris Canonici," 179 pp., 1922.
16. Motry, Rev. Hubert Louis, S.T.D., J.C.D., Diocesan Faculties According to the Code of Canon Law, II-167 pp., 1922.
17. Murphy, Rev. George Lawrence, J.C.D., Delinquencies and Penalties in the Administration and Reception of the Sacraments, IV-121 pp., 1923.
18. O'Reilly, Rev. John Anthony, S.T.B., J.C.D., Ecclesiastical Sepulture in the New Code of Canon Law, II-129 pp., 1923.

19. Michalicka, Rev. Wenceslas Cyrill, O.S.B., J.C.D., Judicial Procedure in Dismissal of Clerical Exempt Religious, 107 pp., 1923.
20. Dargin, Rev. Edward Vincent, S.T.B., J.C.D., Reserved Cases According to the Code of Canon Law, IV-103, pp., 1924.
21. Godfrey, Rev. John A., S.T.B., J.C.D., The Right of Patronage According to the Code of Canon Law, 153 pp., 1924.
22. Hagedorn, Rev. Francis Edward, J.C.D., General Legislation on Indulgences, II-154 pp., 1924.
23. King, Rev. James Ignatius, J.C.D., The Administration of the Sacraments to Dying Non-Catholics, V-141 pp., 1924.
24. Winslow, Rev. Francis Joseph, A.F.M., J.C.D., Vicars and Prefects Apostolic, IV-149 pp., 1924.
25. Correa, Rev. Jose Servelion, S.T.L., J.C.D., La Potestad Legislativa de la Iglesia Catolica, IV-127 pp., 1925.
26. Dugan, Rev. Henry Francis, A.M., J.C.D., The Judiciary Department of the Diocesan Curia, 87 pp., 1925.
27. Keller, Rev. Charles Frederick, S.T.B., J.C.D., Mass Stipends, 167 pp., 1925.
28. Paschang, Rev. John Linus, J.C.D., The Sacramentals According to the Code of Canon Law, 129 pp., 1925.
29. Pointek, Rev. Cyrillus, O.F.M., S.T.B., J.C.D., De Indulto Exclaustrationis necnon Saecularizationis, XIII-289 pp., 1925.
30. Kearney, Rev. Richard Joseph, S.T.B., J.C.D., Sponsors at Baptism According to the Code of Canon Law, IV-127 pp., 1925.
31. Bartlett, Rev. Chester Joseph, A.M., LL.B., J.C.D., The Tenure of Parochial Property in the United States of America, V-108 pp., 1926.
32. Kilker, Rev. Adrian Jerome, J.C.D., Extreme Unction, V-425 pp., 1926.
33. McCormick, Rev. Robert Emmett, J.C.D., Confessors of Religious, VIII-266 pp., 1926.
34. Miller, Rev. Newton Thomas, J.C.D., Founded Masses According to the Code of Canon Law, VII-93 pp., 1926.
35. Roelker, Rev. Edward G., S.T.D., J.C.D., Principles of Privilege According to the Code of Canon Law, XI-166 pp., 1926.
36. Bakalarczyk, Rev. Richardus, M.I.C., J.U.D., De Novitiatu, VIII-208 pp., 1927.
37. Pizzuti, Rev. Lawrence, O.F.M., J.U.L., De Parochis Religiosis, 1927. (Not printed).
38. Bliley, Rev. Nicholas Martin, O.S.B., J.C.D., Altars According to the Code of Canon Law, XIX-132 pp., 1927.
39. Brown, Mr. Brendan Francis, A.B. LL.M., J.U.D., The Canonical Juristic Personality with Special Reference to Its Status in the United States of America, V-212 pp., 1927.

40. Cavanaugh, Rev. William Thomas, C.P., J.U.D., The Reservation of the Blessed Sacrament, VIII-101 pp., 1927.
41. Doheny, Rev. William J., C.S.C., A.B., J.U.D., Church Property: Modes of Acquisition, X-118 pp., 1927.
42. Feldhaus, Rev. Aloysius H., C.PP.S., J.C.D., Oratories, IX-141 pp., 1927.
43. Kelly, Rev. James Patrick, A.B., J.C.D., The Jurisdiction of the Simple Confessor, X-208 pp., 1927.
44. Neuberger, Rev. Nicholas J., J.C.D., Canon 6 or the Relation of the Codex Juris Canonici to the Preceding Legislation, V-95 pp., 1927.
45. O'Keefe, Rev. Gerald Michael, J.C.D., Matrimonial Dispensations, Powers of Bishops, Priests and Confessors, VIII-232 pp., 1927.
46. Quigley, Rev. Joseph A.M., A.B., J.C.B., Condemned Societies, 139 pp., 1927.
47. Zaplotnik, Rev. Johannes Leo, J.C.D., De Vicariis Foraneis, X-142 pp., 1927.
48. Duskie, Rev. John Aloysius, A.B., J.C.D., The Canonical Status of the Orientals in the United States, VIII-196 pp., 1928.
49. Hyland, Rev. Francis Edward, J.C.D., Excommunication, Its Nature, Historical Development and Effects, VIII-181 pp., 1928.
50. Reinmann, Rev. Gerald Joseph, O.M.C., J.C.D., The Third Order Secular of Saint Francis, 201 pp., 1928.
51. Schenk, Rev. Francis J., J.C.D., The Matrimonial Impediments of Mixed Religion and Disparity of Cult, XVI-318 pp., 1929.
52. Coady, Rev. John Joseph, S.T.D., J.U.D., A.M., The Appointment of Pastors, VIII-150 pp., 1929.
53. Kay, Rev. Thomas Henry, J.C.D., Competence in Matrimonial Procedure, VIII-164 pp., 1929.
54. Turner, Rev. Sidney Joseph, C.P., J.U.D., The Vow of Poverty, XLIX-217 pp., 1929.
55. Kearney, Rev. Raymond, A., A.B., S.T.D., J.C.D., The Principles, of Delegation, VII-149 pp., 1929.
56. Conran, Rev. Edward James, A.B., J.C.D., The Interdict, V-163 pp., 1930.
57. O'Neil, Rev. William H., J.C.D., Papal Rescripts of Favor, VII-218 pp., 1930.
58. Bastnagel, Rev. Clement Vincent, J.U.D., The Appointment of Parochial Adjutants and Assistants, XV-257 pp., 1930.
59. Ferry, Rev. William A., A.B., J.C.D., Stole Fees. V-135 pp., 1930.
60. Costello, Rev. John Michael, A.B., J.C.D., Domicile and Quasi-domicile, VII-201 pp., 1930.
61. Kremer, Rev. Michael Nicholas, A.B., S.T.B., J.C.D., Church Support in the United States, VI-1930.

62. Angulo, Rev. Luis, C.M., J.C.D., Legislation de la Iglesia sobre la intencion en la application de la Santa Misa, VII-104 pp., 1931.
63. Frey, Rev. Wolfgang Norbert, O.S.B., A.B., J.C.D., The Act of Religious Profession, VIII-174 pp., 1931.
64. Roberts, Rev. James Brendan, A.B., J.C.D., The Banns of Marriage, XIV-140 pp., 1931.
65. Ryder, Rev. Raymond Aloysius, A.B., J.C.D., Simony, IX-151 pp., 1931.
66. Campagna, Rev. Angelo, Ph.D., J.U.D., Il Vicario Generale del Vescovo, VII-205 pp., 1931.
67. Cox, Rev. Joseph Godfrey, A.B., J.C.D., The Administration of Seminaries, VI-124 pp., 1931.
68. Gregory, Rev. Donald J., J.U.D., The Pauline Privilege, XV-165 pp., 1931.
69. Donohue, Rev. John F., J.C.D., The Impediment of Crime, VII-110 pp., 1931.
70. Dooley, Rev. Eugene A., O.M.I., J.C.D., Church Law On Sacred Relics, IX-143 pp., 1931.
71. Orth, Rev. Raymond Clement, O.M.C., J.C.D., The Approbation of Religious Institutes, 171 pp., 1931.
72. Pernicone, Rev. Joseph M., A.B., J.C.D., The Ecclesiastical Prohibition of Books, XII-267 pp., 1932.
73. Clinton, Rev. Connell, A.B., J.C.D., The Paschal Precept, IX-108 pp., 1932.
74. Donnelly, Rev. Francis B., A.M., S.T.L., J.C.D., The Diocesan Synod, VIII-125 pp., 1932.
75. Torrente, Rev. Camilo, C.M.F., J.C.D., Las Processiones Sagradas, V-145 pp., 1932.
76. Murphy, Rev. Edwin J., C.PP.S., J.C.D., Suspension Ex Informata Conscientia, XI-122, pp., 1932.
77. Mackenzie, Rev. Eric F., A.M., S.T.L., J.C.D., The Delict of Heresy in its Commission Penalization, Absolution, VII-124 pp., 1932.
78. Lyons Rev. Avitus E., S.T.B., J.C.D., The Collegiate Tribunal of First Instance, XI-147 pp., 1932.
79. Connolly, Rev. Thomas A., J.C.D., Appeals, XI-195 pp., 1932.
80. Sangmeister, Rev. Joseph V., A.B., J.C.D., Force and Fear as Precluding Matrimonial Consent, V-211 pp., 1932.
81. Jaeger, Rev. Leo A., A.B., J.C.D., The Administration of Vacant and Quasi-vacant Episcopal Sees in the United States, IX-229 pp., 1932.
82. Rimlinger, Rev. Herbert T., J.C.D., Error Invalidating Matrimonial Consent, VII-79 pp., 1932.
83. Barrett, Rev. John D.M., S.S., J.C.D., A Comparative Study of the Third Plenary Council of Baltimore and the Code, IX-221 pp., 1932.

84. Carberry, Rev. John J., Ph.D., S.T.D., J.C.D., The Juridical Form of Marriage, X-177 pp., 1934.
85. Dolan, Rev. John L., A.B., J.C.D., The Defensor Vinculi, XII-157 pp., 1934.
86. Hannan, Rev. Jerome D., A.M., S.T.D., LL.B., J.C.D., The Canon Law of Wills, IX-517 pp., 1934.
87. Lemieux, Rev. Delisle A., A.M., J.C.D., The Sentence in Ecclesiastical Procedure, IX-131 pp., 1934.
88. O'Rourke, Rev. James J., A.B., J.C.D., Parish Registers, VII-109 pp., 1934.
89. Timlin, Rev. Bartholomew, O.F.M., A.M., J.C.D., Conditional Matrimonial Consent, X-381 pp., 1934.
90. Wahl, Rev. Francis X., A.B., J.C.D., The Matrimonial Impediments of Consanguinity and Affinity, VI-125 pp., 1934.
91. White, Rev. Robert J., A.B., LL.B., S.T.B., J.C.D., Canonical Ante-Nuptial Promises and the Civil Law, VI-152 pp., 1934.
92. Herrera, Rev. Antonio Parra, O.C.D., J.C.D., Legislation Ecclesiastica sobra el Ayuno y la Abstinencia, XI-191 pp., 1935.
93. Kennedy, Rev. Edwin J., J.C.D., The Special Matrimonial Process in Cases of Evident Nullity, X-165 pp., 1935.
94. Manning, Rev. John J., A.B., J.C.D., Presumption of Law in Matrimonial Procedure, XI-111 pp., 1935.
95. Moeder, Rev. John M., J.C.D., The Proper Bishop for Ordination and Dismissorial Letters, VII-135 pp., 1935.
96. O'Mara, Rev. William A., A.B., J.C.D., Canonical Causes For Matrimonial Dispensations, IX-155 pp., 1935.
97. Reilly, Rev. Peter, J.C.D., Residence of Pastors, IX-81 pp., 1935.
98. Smith, Rev. Mariner T., O.P., S.T.L., J.C.D., The Penal Law For Religious, VII-169 pp., 1935.
99. Whalen, Rev. Donald W., A.M., J.C.D., The Value of Testimonial Evidence in Matrimonial Procedure, XIII-297 pp., 1935.
100. Cleary, Rev. Joseph F., J.C.D., Canonical Limitations on the Alienation of Church Property, VIII-141 pp., 1936.
101. Glynn, Rev. John C., J.C.D., The Promoter of Justice, XX-337 pp., 1936.
102. Brennan, Rev. James H., S.S., A.M., S.T.B., J.C.D., The Simple Convalidation of Marriage, VI-135 pp, 1937.
103. Brunini, Rev. Joseph Bernard, J.C.D., The Clerical Obligations of Canons, 139 and 142, X-121 pp., 1937.
104. Connor, Rev. Maurice, A.B., J.C.D., The Administrative Removal of Pastors, VIII-159 pp., 1937.
105. Guilfoyle, Rev. Merlin Joseph, J.C.D., Custom, XI-144 pp., 1937.
106. Hughes, Rev. James Austin, A.B., A.M., J.C.D., Witnesses in Criminal Trials of Clerics, IX-140 pp., 1937.

107. Jansen, Rev. Raymond J., A.B., S.T.L., J.C.D., Canonical Provisions for Catechetical Instruction, VII-153 pp., 1937.

108. Kealy, Rev. John James, A.B., J.C.D,, The Introductory Libellus in Church Court Procedure, XI-121 pp., 1937.

109. McManus, Rev. James Edward, C.SS.R., J.C.D., The Administration of Temporal Goods in Religious Institutes, XVI-196 pp., 1937.

110. Moriarity, Rev. Eugene James, J.C.D., Oaths in Ecclesiastical Courts, X-115 pp., 1937.

111. Rainer, Rev. Eligius George, C.SS.R., J.C.D., Suspension of Clerics, XVII-249 pp., 1937.

112. Reilly, Rev. Thomas F., C.SS.R., J.C.D., Visitation of Religious, VI-195 pp., 1938.

113. Moriarty, Rev. Francis E., C.SS.R., J.C.D., The Extraordinary Absolution from Censures, XV-334 pp., 1938.

114. Connolly, Rev. Nicholas P., J.C.D., The Canonical Erection of Parishes, X-132 pp., 1938.

115. Donovan, Rev. James Joseph, J.C.D., The Pastor's Obligation in Prenuptial Investigation, VII-322 pp., 1938.

116. Harrigan, Rev. Robert J., M.A., S.T.B., J.C.D., The Radical Sanation of Invalid Marriages, VIII-208 pp., 1938.

117. Boffa, Rev. Conrad Humbert, J.C.D., Canonical Provisions for Catholic Schools, VII-211 pp., 1939.

118. Parsons, Rev. Anscar John, O.M. Cap., J.C.D., Canonical Elections, XII-236 pp., 1939.

119. Reilly, Rev. Edward Michael, A.B., J.C.D., The General Norms of Dispensation, X-156 pp., 1939.

120. Ryan, Rev. Gerald Aloysius, A.B., J.C.D., Principles of Episcopal Jurisdiction, XII-172 pp., 1939.

121. Burton, Rev. Francis James, C.S.C., A.B., J.C.D., A Commentary on Canon 1125, X-222 pp., 1940.

122. Miaskiewicz, Rev. Francis Sigismund, J.C.D., Supplied Jurisdiction according to Canon 209, XII-340 pp., 1940.

123. Rice, Rev. Patrick William, A.B., J.C.D., Proof of Death in Prenuptial Investigation, VIII-156 pp., 1940.

124. Anglin, Rev. Thomas Francis, M.S., J.C.D., The Eucharistic Fast, VIII-183 pp., 1941.

125. Coleman, Rev. John Jerome, J.C.D., The Minister of Confirmation, VI-153 pp., 1941.

126. Downs, Rev. John Emmanuel, A.B., J.C.D., The Concept of Clerical Immunity, XI-163 pp., 1941.

127. Esswein, Rev. Anthony Albert, J.C.D., Extrajudicial Penal Powers of Ecclesiastical Superiors, X-144 pp., 1941.

128. Farrell, Rev. Benjamin Francis, M.A., S.T.L., J.C.D., The Rights and Duties of the Local Ordinary Regarding Congregations of Women Religious of Pontifical Approval, V-195 pp., 1941.
129. Feeney, Rev. Thomas John, A.B., S.T.L., J.C.D., Restitution in Integrum, VI-169 pp., 1941.
130. Findlay, Rev. Stephen William, O.S.B., A.B., J.C.D., Canonical Norms Governing the Deposition and Degradation of Clerics, XVII-279 pp., 1941.
131. Goodwine, Rev. John, A.B., S.T.L., J.C.D., The Right of the Church to Acquire Property, VIII-119 pp., 1941.
132. Heston, Rev. Edward Louis, C.S.C., PhD., S.T.D., J.C.D., The Alienation of Church Property in the United States, XII-222 pp., 1941.
133. Hogan, Rev. James John, S.T.L., J.C.D., Judicial Advocates and Procurators, VIII-200 pp., 1941.
134. Kealy, Rev. Thomas M. A.B., Litt.B., J.C.D., Dowry of Women Religious, IX-152 pp., 1941.
135. Keene, Rev. Michael James, O.S.B., J.C.D., Religious Ordinaries and Canon 198.
136. Kerin, Rev. Charles A., S.S., M.A., S.T.B., J.C.D., The Privation of Christian Burial, XVI-279 pp., 1941.
137. Louis, Rev. William Francis, M.A., J.C.D., Diocesan Archives, X-101 pp., 1941.
138. McDevitt, Rev. Gilbert Joseph, A.B., J.C.D., Legitimacy and Legitimation, X-247 pp., 1941.
139. McDonough, Rev. Thomas Joseph, A.B., J.C.D., Apostolic Administrators, X-217 pp., 1941.
140. Meier, Rev. Carl Anthony, A.B., J.C.D., Penal Administrative Procedure Against Negligent Pastors, XI-240 pp., 1941.
141. Schmidt, Rev. John Rogg, A.B., J.C.D., The Principles of Authentic Interpretation in Canon 17 of the Code of Canon Law, XII-331 pp., 1941.
142. Slafkosky, Rev. Andrew Leonard, A.B., J.C.D., The Canonical Episcopal Visitation of the Diocese, X-197 pp., 1941.
143. Swoboda, Rev. Innocent Robert, O.F.M., J.C.D., Ignorance in Relation to the Imputability of Delicts, IX-271 pp., 1941.
144. Dubé, Rev. Arthur Joseph, A.B., J.C.D., The General Principles for the Reckoning of Time in Canon Law. VIII-299 pp., 1941.
145. McBride, Rev. James T., A.B., J.C.D., Incardination and Excardination of Seculars., XX-585 pp., 1941.
146. Król, Rev. John J., J.C.L., The Defendant in Contentious Trials, IX-207 pp., 1942.
147. Comyns, Rev. Joseph J., C.SS.R., J.C.L., The Papal and Episcopal Administration of Church Property.

148. Barry, Rev. Garrett Francis, O.M.I., J.C.L., Violation of the Cloister.
149. Bolduc, Rev. Gatien, C.S.V., A.B., S.T.L., J.C.L., Les études dans les religions cléricales.
150. Boyle, Rev. David John, M.A., J.C.L., The Juridic Effects of Moral Certitude on Pre-Nuptial Guarantees.
151. Canavan, Rev. Walter Joseph, M.A., Litt.D., J.C.L., Profession of Faith.
152. Desrochers, Rev. Bruno, A.B., Ph.L., S.T.B., J.C.L., Le Premier Concile Plénier de Québec et le Code de Droit Canonique.
153. Dillon, Rev. Robert Edward, A.B., J.C.L., Common Law Marriage.
154. Dodwell, Rev. Edward John, Ph.D., S.T.B., J.C.L., The Time and Place for the Celebration of Marriage.
155. Donnellan, Rev. Thomas Andrew, A.B., J.C.L., The Obligation of the Missa pro Populo.
156. Eltz, Rev. Louis Anthony, A.B., JC.L., Cooperation in Crime.
157. Gass, Rev. Sylvester Francis, M.A., J.C.L., Ecclestiastical Pensions.
158. Guiniven, Rev. John Joseph, C.SS.R., J.C.L., The Precept of Hearing Mass on Sundays and Holy Days of Obligation.
159. Gulczynski, Rev. John Theophilus, J.C.L., The Desecration and Violation of Churches.
160. Hammill, Rev. John Leo, M.A., J.C.L., The Obligations of the Traveler according to Canon 14.
161. Haydt, Rev. John Joseph, A.B., J.C.L., Reserved Benefices.
162. Huser, Rev. Roger John, O.F.M., A.B., J.C.L., The Crime of Abortion in Canon Law.
163. Kearney, Rev. Francis Patrick, A.B., S.T.L., J.C.L., The Principles of Canon 1127.
164. Linahen, Rev. Leo James, S.T.L., J.C.L., De Absolutione Complicis in Peccato Turpi.
165. McCloskey, Rev. Joseph Aloysius, A.B., J.C.L., The Subject of Ecclesiastical Law according to Canon 12.
166. O'Neill, Rev. Francis Joseph, C.SS.R., J.C.L., The Dismissal of Religious in Temporary Vows.
167. Prince, Rev. John Edward, A.B., S.T.B., J.C.L., The Diocesan Chancellor.
168. Riesner, Rev. Albert Joseph, C.SS.R., J.C.L., Apostates and Fugitives from Religious Institutes.
169. Stenger, Rev. Joseph Bernard, J.C.L., The Mortgaging of Church Property.
170. Waldron, Rev. Joseph Francis, A.B., J.C.L., The Minister of Baptism.
171. Willett, Rev. Robert Albert, J.C.L., The Probative Value of Documents in Ecclesiastical Trials.
172. Woeber, Rev. Edward Martin, M.A., J.C.L., The Interpellations.

www.ingramcontent.com/pod-product-compliance
Lightning Source LLC
LaVergne TN
LVHW050228080826
844660LV00012B/492

* 9 7 8 0 8 1 3 2 2 3 5 2 0 *